PRODUCTIVITY IN THE ORGANISED MANUFACTURING SECTOR IN INDIA

About the Author

Mihir Kumar Pal is a Senior lecturer in Economics at the Vidyasagar University, Midnapore, West Bengal. He received his undergraduate training and Master's degree from University of Kalyani. He stood First in the First class in both B.A. (Hons.) and M.A. (Economics) and was awarded Gold medals for the same. After obtaining M. Phil (Economics) degree from University of Calcutta, he got his Ph.D. (Economics) degree from Kalyani University in 1997. Dr. Pal has been teaching Econometrics, Indian Economics and Computers in the Department of Economics at Vidyasagar University since 1996. He has published several articles in reputed journals and has presented papers in national and international conferences. Dr. Pal is currently involved in teaching and research in the field of industrial productivity.

PRODUCTIVITY IN THE ORGANISED MANUFACTURING SECTOR IN INDIA

MIHIR KUMAR PAL
Department of Economics,
Vidyasagar University, Midnapore,
West Bengal

CONCEPT PUBLISHING COMPANY, NEW DELHI-110059

ISBN : 81-7022-978-2

First Published 2002

Published and Printed by
Ashok Kumar Mittal
Concept Publishing Company
A/15-16, Commercial Block, Mohan Garden
New Delhi-110059 (India)

Phones: 5351460, 5351794
Fax: 091-(11)-5357103
E-mail: publishing@conceptpub.com

Dedicated to
My Parents

PREFACE

The performance of the manufacturing sector of the Indian economy was particularly dismal during the second half of the sixties and the whole of the seventies. There was a break from this trend during the eighties though the performance during the eighties was by no means superlative. The reason for this performance has been intensively researched.

Research on technological progress during the period has been of special interest. Though this research has not yielded a uniform result, the prevailing opinion seems to be that technological progress during the seventies was very low, if at all positive. Also, it has been argued that there was a break from this trend in the beginning of the eighties. Our study reviews these findings.

Main findings of the present work are not in line with the prevailing opinion. To be more specific, we have found that the total factor productivity growth in the registered manufacturing sector of the Indian economy was quite significant during the seventies and there was, probably, only a marginal improvement in this respect during the eighties. An implication of this finding is that the reason for the dismal performance of the Indian industries, referred to above, cannot be found so much in the lack of technical progress.

Along with the conventional approach we have also taken a somewhat different approach to the estimation of total factor productivity.

MIHIR KUMAR PAL

ACKNOWLEDGEMENTS

This book is a revised version of my Ph.D. dissertation submitted to the University of Kalyani in 1996. In the course of this work I have run into large debts to a number of persons. First of all I must express my gratitude to my supervisor Dr. Madhusudan Datta, who encouraged me all through the present study. I shall remain deeply indebted to him for his constant effort to help me negotiate through the rough terrain of my research field.

I have benefited from comments received from Professor K. L. Krishna of University of Delhi. Earlier version of the work embodied in Chapter IV was presented in a seminar. I am grateful to Professor S. M. Kansal of ISI, Delhi, who had patience enough to go through another version of Chapter IV. I must record a special note of thanks to my teachers Professors A. Sen, S. K. Mukherjee, P. K. Chatterjee and R. N. Bhattacharyya for their suggestions at different stages of the work.

I am also indebted to Mrs. Arundhuti Datta, for many acts of kindness at various stages of my research work. Thanks are also due to many of my friends and colleagues for extending their co-operation to me. Here I must also acknowledge the help and inspiration that I received from my wife, Mita, parents, brothers and other members of our joint family throughout my research work.

I wish to express my gratitude to the authority of Vidyasagar University for providing some financial assistance from UGC unassigned grant for publication. I am thankful to the publisher for their deep interest in bringing out this book.

MIHIR KUMAR PAL

CONTENTS

LIST OF TABLES

Page No.

ABBREVIATIONS USED

TFP	:	Total Factor Productivity
TFPG	:	Total Factor Productivity Growth
L	:	Labour
K	:	Capital
Y	:	Measure of Output (real value added obtained by method described in the text)
Z	:	Measure of Output (real value added obtained by using the GDP deflator)
Y/K	:	Partial Capital Productivity Computed from Y-measure of Output
Y/L	:	Partial Labour Productivity Computed from Y-measure of Output
Z/K	:	Partial Capital Productivity Computed from Z-measure of Output
Z/L	:	Partial Labour Productivity Computed from Z-measure of Output
KEN	:	Kendrick Measure of TFPG
SOLOW	:	Solow Measure of TFPG
TR-lOG	:	Trans-log Measure of TFPG
PROD. FN	:	Production Function Approach to TFPG
CRS	:	Constant Returns to Scale
ASI	:	Annual Survey of Industries
CSO	:	Central Statistical Organisation
NAS	:	National Accounts Statistics
CMI	:	Census of Indian Manufactures
GDP	:	Gross Domestic Product
GNP	:	Gross National Product
GFCF	:	Gross Fixed Capital Formation
INDUSTRY 1	:	Chemical and Chemical Products
INDUSTRY 2	:	Electricity

INDUSTRY 3 : Basic Metal and Alloys
INDUSTRY 4 : Transport Equipment and Parts
INDUSTRY 5 : Electrical Machinery and Parts
INDUSTRY 6 : Non-Electrical Machineries
INDUSTRY 7 : Non-Metallic Mineral Products
INDUSTRY 8 : Cotton Textiles
INDUSTRY 9 : Food Products

1

Introduction

I

The feeling that a substantial part of output growth in the rapidly growing economies is attributable to technological progress has given rise to intensive research on the analysis of productivity growth over the last four decades (Tinbergen 1942, Solow 1957, Denison 1967, Jorgenson and Griliches 1967, 1972, Jorgenson and Christensen 1970, Jorgenson, Christensen and Cummings 1980, Jorgenson and Gallop 1980, etc.). These studies have proposed and chiselled towards perfection new concepts and have opened up an entirely new area of research.

Following the lead, productivity studies for developing economies have also gained momentum. Several such studies have been done for the Indian economy (the most noted among them being Goldar 1986, Ahluwalia 1991, Balakrishnan and Pushpangadan 1994, etc.). The present study is another attempt to understand the role of technological progress in the Indian economy.

Technological progress and total factor productivity are often used synonymously, though there is a conceptual distinction between them. Technological progress is advances in knowledge and its application to the art of production (invention, innovation and diffusion). It may take the form of new goods, new processes or new modes of organisation. On the other hand Total Factor Productivity (TFP), defined as the ratio of output to a weighted combination of inputs, may have substantial gains for a number of reasons other than advances in knowledge. Thus, for example, improvements in the quality of factors (may be caused by spread of education among labourers), economies of scale or better utilisation of capacity may lead to substantial gains in TFP without, in a sense, involving an advance in knowledge. Thus, total factor productivity is a broader concept than technological progress.

Labour productivity and capital productivity give us partial efficiency indices. They are defined as real output per unit of any particular input like labour or capital. Though simplest and easiest to compute, these indices are of great significance in specific contexts. The concept of TFP is more general and uses the concept of combined contribution of factor inputs to the production process. Total Factor Productivity Growth (TFPG) is defined as the difference between the rates of growth of output and the rate of growth of combined inputs (appropriately weighted average of growth of inputs). Generally, the earlier studies have used value shares or income shares as weights. This implies the restrictive assumption of competitive equilibrium and constant returns to scale. Most commonly used TFP indices are the Kendrick index (Kendrick 1961) and Solow index (Solow 1957). In recent studies the trans-log indices of TFP has become most popular (Jorgenson and Lau 1971, 1973, Jorgenson and Gollop 1980, Jorgenson, Christensen and Cummings 1980, Jorgenson and Griliches 1972). The reasons for the popularity is that the underlying production function is very general in nature and is very suitable for discrete data.

II. A BRIEF STUDY OF THE LITERATURE

Productivity studies have shown that a substantial part of output growth in developed economies is attributed to TFP growth (TFPG). Tinbergen (1942), Schmookler (1952), Kendrick (1956) and Solow (1957) have pointed out significant technical progress in the US economy during the late nineteenth and early twentieth century. Fabricant (1954), Abramovitz (1956) and Solow (1957) showed that a major portion of output growth in the US economy could not be explained by growth in factor inputs over the previous decades. Similar findings were also presented for other countries by Kennedy and Thirwall (1972).

Abramovitz (1950), measured the contribution of input growth to output growth by taking share of each input in total output in the base period as the weights. For doing so, he looked at the growth of two catch all inputs, labour and capital. NNP was taken as the measure of output. He assumed labour to be a homogeneous input, thus neglecting skill differences and age-sex-educational composition. Labour was measured in terms of man-hours. He found that, during the period 1869-1878 and 1944-1953, a major portion of output growth in the United States could not be explained by the growth in factor inputs. He calls this residual the growth in productivity of the combined inputs.

Though Solow's period under study (1909-49) was different, his results were similar to those of Abramovitz. He takes up a neoclassical production function with two inputs, capital and labour and a shift variable represented by time. The unit of observation is one year. It is assumed that the effect of technical change is to shift the production function in such a manner as to leave the marginal rate of substitution between capital and labour unchanged, if the capital labour ratio is unchanged, i.e., the technical change is Hicks-neutral. He further assumed that the classification of inputs into capital and labour is exhaustive (sum of the shares is unity). This is equivalent to assuming CRS and marginal product pricing of inputs.

The Solow measure of total factor productivity growth (TFPG) is the difference between he rate of growth of output and the Divisia index of the growth of factors, i.e., the weighted average of the growth rates of factors, the weights being the factor shares. Solow, unlike Abramovitz, takes these weights to be variable. His measure of labour is similar to that of Abramovitz-manhours worked. Solow's measure of capital is not available capital but capital utilised. He allows for under-utilisation of capital stock in times of depression. To do this he multiplies his time series of capital, $K(t)$, by the ratio of employed persons to the total labour force. Solow's results are very similar to those of Abramovitz. It is observed that a large portion (about 80%) of output growth remains to be explained. This residual has been taken to be the contribution of total factor productivity.

Solow (1959) adopted a vintage model of capital to explain the rate of technical change in a study following his study cited above. The first assumption was that machines made this year were a constant percentage rate more productive than machines made last year but still in use this year. Labour working on different machines is assumed to be homogeneous. Second assumption of the model is that, each unit of homogeneous labour input is paid a wage equal to its marginal product regardless of the vintage of machine it works with. Third assumption is that machines of every vintage depreciate at a constant rate.

Jorgenson and Griliches (JG) (1965) have tried to show very carefully the improvement in measurement of total productivity (shift of the production function) by careful weeding out of aggregation and measurement errors.

Taking conventional measures of GNP as output, capital and man-hours, and combining capital and man-hours using constant base period weights, JG derived their first measure of technical change. Input growth explained 52.4 per cent of the total growth in output.

In the second measure, like Solow (1957), used each year's factor share as weights to combine capital and man-hours. Unlike Solow, they disaggregated GNP into consumption goods and investment goods and aggregated them with their share in output to obtain a new index of output growth. It was reported, that input growth could explain 54.3 per cent of the growth in output.

In the third method, JG reached a better measure of capital input by disaggregating the price index of capital. JG obtained disaggregated price indices for structures, equipment and inventories and by careful comparison of input prices with corresponding output price, indices of consumers durables, structures and private consumer expenditure came up with a better measure of capital input. This corrects for bias in input price indices as compared to output price indices. 61.1 per cent of output growth could be explained by input growth following this correction.

In their fourth measure JG have chosen the index of relative utilisation of power sources as an index of capital utilisation and applied Denison's correction in case of labour. This correction for utilisation of factor inputs raised the explanation due to input growth to 71.6 per cent.

Unlike conventional measure, taking into account the flow price of capital services JG further improved upon their measurement of capital input in particular and total productivity in general. Allowing each category of capital input, land, residential and non-residential structures, equipment and inventories, a different depreciation and discount rate, their measure showed input growth to explain 82.7 per cent of output growth.

In a similar fashion, allowing for a flow price of labour input by educational categories JG showed that 96.7 per cent of output growth was explained by the growth in factor inputs.

The above findings probably show that technological progress cannot be isolated from changes in the quality of factors. So, for a serious study of technological progress, the method of measurement of inputs (and also output) is extremely crucial. After JG many studies have been undertaken to measure and compare (internationally and intertemporally) the technological progress of developed as well as developing economies. On the theoretical front many studies have investigated the implications of the use of an aggregate production function (Sato 1975, Diewert 1978, Bruno 1978, Berndt and Christensen, 1973).

For the Indian economy many studies (Reddy and Rao 1962, Singh 1966, Shivamaggi, Rajagopalan and Venkatachalam 1968, Raj Krishnan and Mehta 1968, Banerji 1975) have showed that the contribution of TFP growth to output growth for Indian manufacturing has been very close to nil, even negative. Banerji (1975) presents a significant falling trend in TFP for the period 1946-64. However, Hashim and Dadi (1973), Narasimham and Fabrycy (1974) and others have found a significant rising trend in TFP for the above period and they are of the view that about fifty per cent of output growth was contributed by TFPG. Recent studies (Goldar 1986, Ahluwalia 1991, Balakrishnan and Pushpangadan 1994) have pointed out that productivity or efficiency of the manufacturing sector of the economy have not improved over time in spite of significant expansion of the manufacturing sector and rise in the share of manufacturing in total output. Goldar (1986) analysed productivity trends in Indian manufacturing during 1951-79. This study incorporated a methodological improvement for the measurement of TFP — the trans-log index of TFP for Indian industries. Goldar, points out that TFPG in Indian manufacturing during 1951-79 has been rather sluggish and relative contribution of TFPG to output growth quite small. Ahluwalia (1991) found poor performance of the Indian manufacturing with respect to the TFPG upto the end of seventies. However, she indicated a phenomenon of turnaround (a turn form a falling to a rising trend) in the first-half of eighties. She also went into an international comparison of productivity estimates between India and other developing economies. Hong Kong, Singapore, Taiwan, Korea, Argentina, Thailand and Indonesia have done much better than India's negligible growth in TFP over the two decades 60s and 70s. In spite of improvement in the 80s long term TFPG from 1959-60 to 1985-86 compares unfavourably with similar estimates available for other economies. This study also hints at lower TFPG for industries with higher capital labour ratio. Taking into account the changes in relative prices of inputs and outputs in the estimation of value added for aggregate manufacturing of the Indian economy, Balakrishnan and Pushpangadan (1994) arrived at results which negate the turnaround hypothesis. This study points out that productivity growth in the 1980s may actually have been slower than in the earlier decade.

Bannerji's (1975) study is comprehensive and covers aggregate manufacturing over the period 1948-64. He pays attention to the problem of working out a series of capital input in constant prices from book value figures on capital available in CMI and ASI publications. Hashim and Dadi (1973) covers the period 1946-64. They construct a capital input series in constant prices utilising all available data. Goldar (1986) after a thorough review of the studies by Bannerji (1975) and Hashim and Dadi (1973) has come to the conclusion that the differences in the estimates of TFP change between these two studies can be traced to the differences in the capital series and the underlying assumptions. On account of the observed differences, Goldar re-estimated the capital series on the basis of more plausible assumptions and used the series for the calculation of TFP change for the period 1951-65.

Ahluwalia (1985) has obtained Solow and trans-log measures of TFP at different levels of industrial aggregation for the period 1959-80 and for the sub-periods 1959-65 and 1966-80. She presents four alternative estimates of TFPG for the whole manufacturing industry and for the use based and input based classification of industries. Of these, one relates to the Solow measure and three to the trans-log measure. The three trans-log measures differ among themselves slightly in regard to the capital stock series used. The estimates of TFPG over the period 1959-80 for aggregate manufacturing range between –0.2 and 0.3 for two different measures of trans-log indices. Goldar's (1986) estimate of 1.3 per cent per annum for the category of large and medium establishments in the registered manufacturing for the period 1959-79 is significantly different from that of Ahluwalia (1985).

According to Krishna (1987) the difference between Goldar's and Ahluwalia's estimate may be due to the following reasons :

(a) Difference in the estimates of capital stock for initial year (bench-mark year) used in the perpetual inventory method.
(b) The method of deflation of investment and initial capital stock figures : while Goldar has adopted the deflators at the aggregate industry level, Ahluwalia has taken the trouble of applying the deflators at the level of two digit industries and then arriving at the aggregate capital stock series for the total industry or industry groups by suitable summation.
(c) Goldar's estimate covers industries 511 (electric light and power) and 512 (gas manufacturing and distribution) while Ahluwalia's estimates excludes these for manufacturing.
(d) Ahluwalia has taken much greater care in correcting value added series for price changes.

With regard to the trend in capital-output ratios following important studies may be cited. Ahluwalia (1985) examines trends in capital-output ratio over the period 1959-80 for the manufacturing sector and obtained statistically significant trend. Thus, specifically, a falling trend in capital productivity and generally a falling trend in TFP is noticed for this period.

Panchamukhi (1986) opposed a general view that inefficiency of capital investment in India has increased over the period 1976-79. He has carried out a detailed econometric analysis for manufacturing and other sectors, in the process of arriving at such a view.

Brahmananda (1982) obtained productivity ratios, partial and total, for the year 1960-61, 1970-71 and 1980-81 with 1950-51 as base. He found that the productivity performance during 1971-81 was worse than in the earlier two decades. Significant limitations of his work are that, it is based on data for four time points only and again, the full details of the construction of the data series are not available.

At the end it may be said that there are basically two important estimates of TFPG for the organised manufacturing sector for the period 1960-80. According to one estimate TFPG is 1.3 per cent per annum and according to the other it lies between –0.6 to 0.3 per cent. Sound logical justification of this difference in the estimates of TFPG is yet to be found. Other studies, though not methodologically sound, suggest a decline in TFPG for the above period.

III. THE PRESENT STUDY

The primary objective of this study is to analyse productivity trend in the organised manufacturing sector in India over the time period 1970-71 to 1987-88. We have also tried to estimate the contributions of TFPG and the growth of employment of combined inputs towards the growth of output. Nine major industry groups, at the two digit level, constituting approximately 80 per cent of the value added in manufacturing sector in 1982-83, at current prices have been taken up for this study.

We have estimated TFPG in four different ways. The Kendrick, Solow and Trans-log indices have been computed and compared with one another. Then we have used the production function approach. In this approach we have estimated the underlying production function using the general trans-log framework and used the estimated coefficients of the production function to obtain estimates of TFPG. Here we have deviated from the approach commonly followed in the literature. In case of the measurement of output, we have worked with two alternative estimates. This helps us to see how susceptible the estimates of TFP are to the estimates of output. Then we have compared TFPG estimates obtained by all the above mentioned approaches. The industries have been ranked according to TFPG and rank correlations, for different sets of rankings from different measures, computed.

We have discussed the concept of productivity and the methodology adopted in the present study for measuring total factor productivity growth in Chapter 2. This chapter, not only presents the conventional approaches to the measurement of TFPG, but also explains in detail the methodology adopted by us in the present study. The limitations of the conventional measures as well as that of the production function approach adopted in the present study have been discussed. Measurement of the relevant variables and data sources are discussed in the last section of this chapter. Our approach to the measurement of Kendrick, Solow and Trans-log indices of TFPG and their estimates are presented in the first-two sections of Chapter 3. An account of the behaviour of TFPG during the 70s and the 80s is made in Section III of this chapter. Section IV makes a comparative analysis of our estimates of TFPG *vis-a-vis* those obtained by previous studies. A discussion on the ranking or industries according to TFPG obtained from different measures and their corresponding rank correlation coefficients is made in section V.

Chapter 4 deals with the computation of TFPG through the estimation of production function. While section I presents a brief overview of the approach undertaken by us, TFPG estimates from the direct estimation of production function (based on the general trans-log production function) is presented in the next section. A brief comparison of TFPG estimates obtained from two different measures of real value added, computed through regression exercises, is made in section III of this chapter. Changes in TFPG estimates over the two sub-periods (1970-71 to 1980-81 and 1981-82 to 1987-88) for both the real value added measures are shown in section IV. In section V we have gone into a comparison of our estimates of TFPG with those obtained by the earlier similar studies. An investigation into the joint contribution of factor inputs and TFPG, towards the growth in output, is made in section VI of this very chapter. Section I of Chapter 5 discusses the significance of the partial productivity indices and present the estimates of these indices. This section besides analysing the trend in labour and capital productivity, also presents the trend in capital intensity. For the rest of this chapter, we have tried to make a detailed comparison between the estimates of TFPG obtained through various approaches as presented in Chapters 3 and 4. Specifically, section II goes into the comparison between the different measures with respect to average annual TFPG. An account of the direction and magnitude of changes in TFPG during the seventies and the eighties, for different approaches, is made in section III. Differences in the estimates of the contribution of inputs and TFPG towards output growth and ranking of industries according to TFPG are focused in section IV. Chapter 6 summarises the findings of the study and draws the conclusion.

2

Methodology

I

Productivity may be defined as the ratio of the output of a commodity measured in real terms to that of one or more of the inputs used, also measured in real terms. This definition is a very crude one but captures the essential concept. We can modify the measure by forming quality adjusted productivity indices to account for the differences in quality of similar products and factors. In productivity analysis the concept of Total Factor Productivity (TFP) is widely used, which is defined as the ratio of real output to a weighted combination of real inputs, standing for the index of total input. Thus total factor productivity refers to that portion of output growth which is not directly explained by the growth in the inputs.

Empirical studies show that growth in output cannot be totally explained simply by the growth in the two aggregate factor of production capital input and labour input. The residual growth of output, that cannot be explained by the growth of these two inputs, is caused by a host of influences that are difficult to categorise precisely. Denison calls it the measure of our ignorance (Denison, 1967). This 'residual factor' is supposed to cause the growth in total factor productivity (TFPG). TFPG is also loosely referred to as a measure of technical change.

Technological progress, though often used interchangingly with TFPG, may, strictly speaking, be distinguished from the latter. Technological progress is often thought of as advances in knowledge and its application relating to the art of production (invention, innovation and diffusion). It may take the form of new goods, new processes or new modes of organisation.[1] On the other hand, changes in TFP, as defined above, may take place for a number of reasons other than (or at least not immediately connected with) advances in knowledge or its application as such. Thus, improvement in the quality or labour, economies of scale or better utilisation of capacity may lead to substantial gains in TFP without always involving an advance in technical knowledge. For example, an improvement in the work culture or structural adjustment may lead to such gains. While it is important to keep the distinction in mind, it may not be highly rewarding in practice to make the distinction.

The simplest measure of productivity is the partial productivity defined as real output per unit of any particular real input like labour or capital. Such measures are easiest to compute and interpret. Partial productivity indices are of great interest in specific contexts of analyses. However, since several factors are combined to give output one naturally desires to have some composite index of productivity, an index which is not specific to a single factor, rather depends on the totality of factors.

In productivity analysis the concept of total factor productivity growth (TFPG) is widely used today.[2] Basically the concept is to treat output as a function of factors of production, capital (K) and labour (L), as well as some unknown influence captured by a proxy variable, time (T).

$$Y = F(K, L, T).$$

Then, TFPG, $G = \frac{1}{Y}\frac{\delta Y}{\delta T}$. There are several approaches to the measurement of 'G'. These are based on production functions of different levels of generality. 'G' can be expressed in terms of factor elasticities and factor growth rates (discussed below). Direct estimation of production function to obtain factor elasticities is not commonly undertaken. The common approach is to equate the factor prices with the respective marginal productivity so that factor shares in output are the respective elasticities. The factor shares are easily observable. So, the estimation of the production function can be avoided.

The above approach is extremely convenient and probably reasonably efficient for economies which approximate to some extent the underlying optimising assumptions of competitive equilibrium economics. Since resources are allocated efficiently each factor is paid just the marginal product. Further, there exists constant returns to scale (CRS) so that payment according to marginal productivity exhausts the product. The assumptions may not be too far out of the way for developed economies which probably operate at a certain high level of efficiency in resource allocations. Constancy of returns to scale, though not often true, has sometimes been found a more or less reasonable approximation to reality.

However, for an underdeveloped economy like India it seems too much to pre-assume allocative efficiency in the study of the trend of total factor productivity. A large part of the registered manufacturing sector being under the public sector with administered product prices and the employment (both of capital and labour) policy not often being particularly related to the criterion of profit maximization (Dutt 1987), the presumption of a primary level of allocative efficiency seems invalid. For various reasons (e.g., lack of freedom of entry or exit) the allocative efficiency may not be the hallmark of the private sector also. So, estimates of total factor productivity based on the equality of factor shares to the respective elasticities are likely to be highly biased (probably negatively, because of inefficiency in the use of factors even though there is improvement of techniques) for India.[3]

In fact, if the profit maximization criterion is not adhered to one need not be surprised to find the marginal productivity for some factor for some industry to be close to zero or even negative. This may be so, for example, when the employment of a factor cannot be trimmed even though demand for the product is low or, even, when the employment policy is determined beyond the plant level based on criteria unrelated to profit maximisation (Joshi and Little, 1994) or, more generally, productive efficiency. However, in spite of such 'inefficiency', it may still be found that TFPG is positive. This may be because of the application of advanced scientific techniques, the economy of scale or some other reason like an improvement in management in some respect. Clearly, in view of the inappropriateness of the assumptions mentioned above it may be questioned how far they can contribute to the efficiency of the resulting estimates.

Before we go on to discuss the different measures of TFPG we should mention some general problems associated with them. All the measures of TFPG are based on the concept of aggregate production function. Value added is taken as the measure of output. But the existence of an aggregate production function requires that the technology is separable in value added, which may be taken as a function of capital, labour and the level of technology. Further, the sectoral value added functions as well as the functions relating capital and labour inputs to their components must be identical for all sectors. As regards prices, perfect competition should prevail in the factor markets for each component. If the separability condition is relaxed the use of real value added for real output in the production function. If the separability condition is relaxed the use of real value added for output in the production function requires that the prices of output and material inputs should move in the same proportion (Berndt and Christensen, 1974; Diewert, 1978; Jorgenson, 1991).

Obviously the above conditions are heavily restrictive even when one is concerned with studies disaggregated to the level of industries, like the present one. But the problems have not deterred econometricians from using even aggregate production function. Jorgenson (1991) has attempted to estimate the magnitude of error that the assumption of an aggregate production function entails. He has concluded that for the analysis of long run trend the error involved is not serious, though not negligible. However the approach may be misleading if the purpose is to distinguish productivity trends over short periods. It should be useful to keep the above points in mind in the study of TFPG.[4]

II. MEASURES OF TFPG

In the present study we have used four measures of TFPG. An

index of TFP can in general be written symbolically as :

$$A = \frac{Y}{\alpha L + \beta K} \tag{1}$$

where *A*, *Y*, *L* and *K* are respectively the index of total factor productivity, real output, labour and real capital inputs. α, β stand for appropriate weights of labour and capital inputs often taken as the wage and rental rates. TFPG is the rate of growth of *A*, or, dA/A.

The Kendrick Measure

The Kendrick index is structured implicitly on the assumption of a linear production function homogeneous in capital and labour and payment according to marginal productivity. The index is given by:

$$A_t^k = \frac{Y_t}{w_o L_t + r_o K_t} \tag{2}$$

Obviously, if the assumptions are valid $A_o^k = 1$. The Kendrick formula for TFPG which adjusts for the deviations from constant returns to scale and uses a moving base (Nadiri, 1970) is given by:

$$G_1^k = \frac{Y_1 / Y_0}{\left(wL_1 + rK_1\right) / \left(wL_0 + rK_0\right)} - 1 \tag{3}$$

We have used this formula to compute the Kendrick measure. Only, it should be mentioned here that the Kendrick measure can also be computed by using (2) and then finding out the growth rates.

The Solow Measure

Solow (1957) proceeds to obtain a measure of technical progress by explicitly introducing a time variable in the production function to stand for technical progress. Then for simplicity he assumes

Hicks-neutral technical progress so that the production function takes the special form:

$$Y = A(t) f(K,L) \tag{4}$$

The multiplicative factor $A(t)$ represents shifts over time. Differentiating with respect to time and dividing by Y we get

$$\frac{\dot{Y}}{Y} = \frac{\dot{A}}{A} + \frac{S_K \dot{K}}{K} + \frac{S_l \dot{L}}{L} \tag{5}$$

where $S_k = (\delta Y/\delta K)(K/Y)$ and $S_l = (\delta Y/\delta L)(L/Y)$. Now from the time series of the rates of growth or output (Y) capital (K) and Labour (L) and those of factor shares S_k and S_l one can find out estimates of TFPG given by $\dot{A}/A$ Here we may mention that the assumption of just two factors of production means that $S_k = 1 - S_l$. The assumption of equality of factor payments with respective marginal productivities then implies constant returns to scale. Thus Solow index of TFPG in fact has the assumption of a linear homogeneous production function with Hicks neutral technological progress. For real life estimation problems time is necessarily discrete and the growth rates should, therefore, be the change over a unit period of time divided by the original value. However we have deviated from this norm and taken the growth rates to be the difference between the logarithms of the variables concerned. This is a valid approximation so long as the period is small. Further, we have fitted a semi-logarithmic trend over the time series of labour shares for each industry. Where a significant trend is not found the arithmetic mean is taken as the constant labour share for the industry. Where a significant trend exists the fitted values are used as the shares for the respective periods. Thus finally we can write the Solow measure of TFPG as the difference between the rate of growth of output and the Divisia index of the growth of factors, i.e., the weighted average of the growth rates of factors, the weights being the factor shares.

$$G^s = \frac{\dot{A}}{A} = \frac{\dot{Y}}{Y} - \left(S_k \frac{\dot{K}}{K} + S_l + \frac{\dot{L}}{L} \right) \tag{6}$$

It may be mentioned here that the assumption of homogeneity of degree one with Hicks-neutral technological progress has often led to the presumption that the Solow index is based on the Cobb-Douglas production function. The implication is that the factor shares are constant though, of course, Solow himself did not use a constant factor share in his estimation. Our procedure has been to use the trend values of factor shares which meant the use of constant shares in seven out of nine industries which showed no significant trend. Our justification of the procedure is two-fold. Firstly, we wanted to keep the Solow measure distinct from the trans-log measure (discussed below).5 Secondly, we felt that the observed factor shares often do not reflect the marginal productivities and involve significant measurement error (the feeling has been largely ignored in the case of trans-log measure which explicitly assumes factor shares to be functions of time).

The Trans-log Measure

The trans-log measure is based on a very flexible form of production function that is particularly suitable for application to observations at discrete points. The second property in particular has made the measure widely popular. We may derive the trans-log production function:

$$\log Y = \alpha_0 + \alpha_1 \log K + \alpha_2 \log L + \alpha_3 T + \frac{1}{2}\left(\beta_{11} \log^2 K + \beta_{22} \log^2 L + \beta_{33} T^2\right) + \beta_{12} \log K \log L + \beta_{13} \log K.T + \beta_{23} \log L.T \quad (7)$$

where Y, K and L are output, capital stock and labour employed and T stands for time. Measurement of the variables has been discussed below. We have also introduced a dummy variable in the following form :

$$\log Y = \alpha_0 + \alpha Dt + \alpha_1 \log K + \alpha_2 \log L + \alpha_3 T + \frac{1}{2}(\beta_{11} \log^2 K + \beta_{22} \log^2 L + \beta_{33} T^2) + \beta_{12} \log K \log L + \beta_{13} \log K.T + \beta_{23} \log L.T \quad (8)$$

This dummy variable takes into account a shift in TFPG. Elasticities of output with respect to K, L and T are:

$$V_K = \alpha_1 + \beta_{11} \log K + \beta_{12} \log L + \beta_{13} T \tag{9}$$

$$V_L = \alpha_2 + \beta_{22} \log L + \beta_{12} \log K + \beta_{23} T \tag{10}$$

$$V_T = \alpha_3 + \alpha D + \beta_{33} T + \beta_{13} \log K + \beta_{23} \log L \tag{11}$$

For discrete time the contributions of specific inputs and total factor productivity to growth of output can be obtained as follows:

$$\frac{\dot{Y}}{Y} = \overline{V}_K \frac{\dot{K}}{K} + \overline{V}_L \frac{\dot{L}}{L} + \overline{V}_T \tag{12}$$

where,

$$(\dot{Y}/Y)_t = \log Y_t - \log Y_{t-1}$$
$$(\dot{K}/K)_t = \log K_t - \log K_{t-1}$$
$$(\dot{L}/L)_t = \log L_t - \log L_{t-1} \tag{13}$$

Further

$$\overline{V}_{K,t} = \tfrac{1}{2}\left(V_{K,t} + V_{K,t-1}\right)$$
$$\overline{V}_{L,t} = \tfrac{1}{2}\left(V_{L,t} + V_{L,t-1}\right)$$
$$\overline{V}_{T,t} = \tfrac{1}{2}\left(V_{T,t} + V_{T,t-1}\right) \tag{14}$$

[To simplify notations a bit we have excluded time subscripts from elasticities in equation (12).]

V_T is the Divisia quantity index of total factor productivity growth (or technical change) applied to the trans-log production function, or the trans-log measure of TFPG. Whereas the first-two terms on the right hand side of (12) are the contributions of capital and labour to output growth, so the sum of the two terms represent the contribution of inputs to output growth.

The use of conditions of producer's equilibrium facilitates the computation of TFPG. The assumptions that factors are paid their marginal products and production shows constant returns to scale mean that the necessary conditions of producer's equilibrium are given by the equality of value shares and the respective elasticity.

$$\text{Thus,} \qquad V_K = \frac{\delta \log Y}{\delta \log K} = \frac{p_K K}{p_Y Y} = S_K$$

$$\text{Similarly,} \quad V_L = \frac{\delta \log Y}{\delta \log L} = \frac{p_L L}{p_Y Y} = S_L$$

Where P and S represent price and value share.

The value shares are easily observed. Also, the rates of growth of output, capital and labour can be obtained from the respective time series. Substituting observed S_k, S_L (after centring) for $\overline{V}_K, \overline{V}_L$ in equation (12) one can find a measure of total factor productivity. It is this particular measure, rather than the general form referred to above, that has come to be known as the transcendental logarithmic (trans-log) measure of TFPG. It may be observed here that since the observed factor shares relate to the end of the period a two period average is taken to centre it to the middle of the period. So the difference between the Solow index and the trans-log index boils down to the use of a constant or trend value of factor shares in the former case and the observed (centred) factor shares in the latter case.[6]

Clearly, the trans-log measure uses the assumption of constant returns to scale and is, therefore, deprived of some of the flexibility of the trans-log production function. Further, the measure assumes that the factors are paid their marginal products and is, therefore, subject to the limitations referred to above. It should, therefore, be interesting to study how the measure compares with the more general (with its own limitations) measure where the parameters are obtained from the production function fitted to the observed data. We have called the latter index the production function index. Thus the production function index does not equate the factor elasticities with the respective observed factor shares. The elasticities are obtained from the fitted production function. We have estimated both the trans-log and the production function indices.

In order to obtain the production function index of TFPG we have undertaken direct estimation of the trans-log production function.[7] Our approach, if somewhat 'inefficient' from the econometric point of view (discussed below), avoids the assumptions of constant returns to scale or producer's equilibrium leading to the use of income shares as measures of factor elasticity. The problem is that direct estimation of trans-log production function involves estimation of a large number of parameters based on basically three time series observations, and that too, of poor quality. This surely affects the efficiency of estimates. But instead of putting artificial restrictions on parameters in the form of assumptions of constant returns to scale or Hicks-neutral technical progress or using the equilibrium equations, we excluded step by step through the process of backward elimination, taking one parameter at a time, generally (but not always in a straightforward way) those parameters which were found to be insignificant in regression exercises. We now describe in detail the procedure by which we obtain our estimates of the production function and the measure of TFPG.

In the first stage we first estimate the general trans-log production function using ordinary least squares procedures and all the observations we have. Almost invariably this resulted in very low values of t-statistics for almost all the coefficients and very high R^2 of estimation. Then we excluded one term of the production function (equivalent to the assumption that the relevant coefficient is not significantly different from zero). Normally, dropping a bottom ranking term (with respect to t-values) gives the best result. The process is repeated in the next step starting normally with the best or the second or even the third or next best result (use of personal judgement is inevitable) of the previous step. We proceed in this way until we reach a result where all the coefficients have t-statistics significant at the 5 per cent level. It is important to note here that we have *ignored those regressions which do not contain all the variables K, L and T in some form or other.* We have often obtained more than one result or in some cases even no result (because we did not consider all the possible combinations of terms) for which all the coefficients have significant t-statistics. Then we repeated the whole process leaving one observation from the beginning, then one observation from the end and then one observation both from the beginning and the end. Sometimes we tried by dropping two observations from the beginning or the end. Ultimately we obtained for each industry a number or results with all the coefficients significant at 5 per cent level. We call such a result a good result.

In the second stage we checked each good result whether it remains good in each of the three cases: (i) when all the observations are considered, (ii) when one observation is excluded from the beginning and (iii) when one observation is excluded from the end. We call the good results which remain good in all the three above cases (observationally) 'robust' results.

In the third stage we subject each of the robust results to F-test to check whether all the excluded coefficients are jointly insignificant. We ignore the robust results that fail the F-test. The F-test is given by :

$$F_{\mathrm{q,n-k}} = \frac{R_{\mathrm{g}}^2 - R_{\mathrm{c}}^2}{1 - R_{\mathrm{g}}^2} \cdot \frac{n-k}{q}$$

(Where n, k and q are respectively the number of observations, the number of coefficients in the general form of the production function and number of independent linear restrictions, i.e., the number of coefficients assumed zero in the present case.)

The robust results passing the F-test have then been used to compute the contribution of inputs (capital and labour taken together, as discussed above). Our presumption is that in spite of significant sources of inefficiency, as discussed above, the joint contribution of inputs taken together should not be negative over the whole of roughly the two decades. We have found that in some of the cases the regression results passing the first-three stages show a negative contribution of capital and labour taken together. We have ignored such results and presented only results that pass all the above criteria. However, in one case we have not found any result showing positive contributions of inputs. In this case we present the result which shows maximum (though negative) contribution of inputs. Finally, these results have been used to compute the production function measure of TFPG following equations (11) and (13).

In order to obtain average TFPG over a period of time we have taken the arithmetic mean of annual estimates for both TFPG and contribution of inputs to growth of output. Then these averages have been adjusted to the growth rate of output as the growth of output must be equal to the sum of TFPG and the contribution of inputs (equation 12).

III. DATA AND VARIABLES

As mentioned above we have taken real value added as the relevant measure of output in the present study. Computation of the index of real value added (ASI provides value added at current prices only) involves some important considerations which have been discussed in Balakrishnan and Pushpangadan (1994). Ahluwalia (1991) computes real value added by deflating the current price value added by the wholesale price indices. Balakrishnan and Pushpangadan (1994), however, computes the real value added by deflating output and material inputs separately by the respective prices and then arrived at results not clearly supporting Ahluwalia's results. The authors have concluded that the movement of the relative price of intermediate input provides the crucial explanation for Ahluwalia's result of turnaround in TFPG. This highlights the crucial nature of the estimation problem.

We have used two alternative measures of real value added in our study. The first is obtained by the use of a simple value added deflator straightaway instead of the wholesale price index. NAS provides estimates of real value added in the manufacturing sector as a whole, but this is arrived at by using a single wholesale price index deflator. Thus we could not use the ratio between the current and constant price value added in manufacturing (as in NAS) as the price index of value added in the sector. So we used the GDP deflator obtained from NAS as the ratio between current price and constant price GDP. In our view this index, though not satisfactory, may not be worse than the whole sale price index for our purpose. The use of the GDP deflator is apparently too simplistic a solution. But it is not clear that we are more correct when we deflate by the wholesale price index for even the particular industrial product. Because the inputs and outputs are different products. The ideal, of course, is to take separate and specific price indices to deflate inputs and output. But that is too large a task for the present study.[8]

In fact the GDP deflator shows a trend somewhat steeper than that for the wholesale price of manufacturing. So the value added growth rate obtained by us is lower than what would be obtained by using a wholesale price index for manufacturing. It seemed to us interesting and worthwhile to work with this deflator. The value added series for different industries obtained by deflation with GDP deflator has been designated as 'Z'. The Z-measure of value added is admittedly a crude one particularly because it uses a single GDP deflator to deflate value added of all the different industries. Thus the Z-measure implicitly treats the value added by different industries as homogeneous. So far as value added is taken as a measure of industry output this is not defensible.

Our second alternative, which in our view is a better one, is to use a modified value added index. This is represented as, $Y_t = Y_0 I_t$, where Y_t is the real value added index for the year 't' for any particular industry, Y_0 represents value added in the particular industry for a benchmark year. We have taken 1981-82 as the benchmark year as it is the base of the wholesale price index used here. Further, 1981-82 is more or less the central point of the time period under study. I_t represent the index of real output for time 't', $I_t = I_t^0 / I_0^0$, where I_t^0 is the value of output in period 't' at prices of '0'. Relevant data are obtained from Annual Survey of Industries, National Accounts Statistics and Report on Currency and Finance. The '*Y*' series discussed above avoids the problem relating to the measurement of relative price of inputs. However, the implicit assumption in this case is that real value added is proportional to real output and, hence, real input is proportional to real output. The '*Y*' series will be based to the extent the assumption of proportionality is invalid. In the context of the study of technological change this assumption implies that technological change concerns the efficiency of factors like capital and labour, not material inputs.

As for the measurement of labour input, Kendrick (1973) considers all workers within each industry to be homogeneous. He totally neglects the influence of labour quality on the measurement of industry's labour input. Denison (1974) is of the view that disaggregation by characteristics is essential in measuring labour input. He also points out that earnings can be used in weighting the components of labour input only if the average earnings for different categories of labour input cross classified by education or by age and sex are proportional to the corresponding marginal products. 'Total employees' as a measure of labour input includes both workers and persons other than workers. The latter category of employees includes supervisors, technicians, managers, clerks and other similar types of employees. If we take 'total employees' as the measure of labour input then we would be guided by the assumption that 'workers' and 'persons other than workers' are perfectly substitutable. The above assumption is unrealistic as is pointed out by Griliches (1967). Further, he adds that efficiency differences in different classes of labourers are reflected in their rates of remuneration.

In the context of Indian economy, all the major works on productivity of the manufacturing sector, such as Goldar (1986), Ahluwalia (1991), Balakrishnan and Pushpangadan (1994), considers 'total employees' as the measure of labour input. In majority of the earlier studies, 'number of workers' or 'number of employees' has been used as the measure of labour input. In the studies of Sastry (1966) and Sankar (1970) attempts have been made to take into account quality changes of different components of labour by weighting them by their wage share. Goldar (1986), talks of imperfections of the labour market and the inappropriateness of the assumption of efficiency of different categories of labour being reflected in their rates of remuneration in the Indian context.

In our present study we have made the uncomfortable assumption that efficiency differences in different classes of labour are largely reflected in their remunerations. Although we are convinced that the assumption is not particularly valid for a country like India, the alternative of treating labour as homogeneous also involves serious error. Thus, admittedly, our labour index is not very satisfactory but, probably, it is better than an unweighted sum of different categories of labour.[9] 'Workers' and 'other employees' (includes supervisors, technicians, managers etc.) are the two groups of labour, data are consistently available for the period under study. Labour index is formed by a weighted sum of the number of heads in these two groups, weights being the relative group remunerations. Relevant data is obtained from Annual Survey of Industries and Indian Labour Statistics.

The estimation of the capital stock, apart from the theoretical problems regarding the very concept (Robinson, J. 1970, Garegnani, 1970) is a tricky job. The treatment of capital as a factor of production became the central issue in an extended debate among Denison (1957, 1966, 1972), Griliches and Jorgenson (1966), Jorgenson (1980, 1989) and Kendrick (1961, 1973). The state of the debate is well summarised in Diewart (1980). For the Indian economy two important studies are by Banerji (1975) and the other by Hashim and Dadi (1973).

We have not taken into account, working capital so far as the measurement of capital is concerned. In this regard Sinha and Sawhney (1970) argues, as quoted in Goldar (1986), "While the importance of working capital to industrial productivity cannot be denied, the inventory and cash holdings are more often determined by supply and market expectations than technological pipeline requirements and have, therefore; far less bearing on productivity than fixed investment. Also the available data on inventories and cash are as on the last day of the year and not the average holding of working capital though the year which alone may be appropriately related to the annual follow of output." In this respect Banerji (1975) talks of the difficulty of arriving at a suitable price index required for deflation purpose.

Many intricate issues come out with regard to the choice between gross and net stock of capital. Most of the studies favoured gross stock on the ground that the net value declines much rapidly then the ability of a capital good to contribute to production. Denison (1967) is of the view that the correct index of capital services would lie somewhere between the gross and net stocks and advocates a weighted average of the two. In this regard Goldar (1986) points out that the available data is too crude to make a proper estimate of capital consumption and hence of net capital stock for Indian industries. This has also been pointed out by Sinha and Sawhney (1970), Banerji (1975) and others who argue that the figures on depreciation presented in Census of Manufacturing Industries and Annual Survey of Industries are calculated at the rates allowed by income tax authorities and rarely represent the true capital consumption.

Kendrick (1973) and Denison (1974) have strongly argued against any correction of capital stock figures for underutilisation of capacity in productivity analysis. They are of the view that the degree of capacity utilisation reflects the degree of efficiency of enterprises and hence would be incorporated in the changes in productivity indices. In addition to the conceptual intricacies, Goldar (1986) points out the poor quality of data on capacity utilisation.

Since the study by Goldsmith in 1951, most of the studies have used the perpetual inventory method (PIM) for estimating capital input. For the Indian case, recent important studies such as Goldar (1986) and Ahluwalia (1991), have used some variant of the PIM. In this method the capital stock of a given year is traced to the stream of past investments at constant prices. PIM requires an estimate of the capital stock for a benchmark year and estimates of investment in the subsequent periods. Let K_0 denote the benchmark year real capital stock and I_t the real gross investment in fixed capital in the year 't' and let 'r' be the annual rate of discarding of assets. Then K_t, real gross fixed capital stock for the year 't' is obtained as follows :

$$K_t = K_0 + \sum_{t=1}^{t} I(t)$$

where $I(t) = I_t - rK_{t-1}$.

Goldar (1986) talks of various possibilities with regard to the rate of discarding of assets. This may be zero, a constant or a fraction of previous year's fixed capital stock.

The Central Statistical Organisation has recently been engaged in the estimation of capital stock by the perpetual inventory method (CSO, 1989). But the results of the project are not yet available. The estimates given by ASI are basically book values which use depreciation rates allowed by the income tax authorities. We have not gone into the problem in detail to obtain alternative estimates. So, clearly, there is scope for improvement in the data. It should be interesting to note how results vary with alternative estimates. A trans-log index of capital stock should be of particular interest. Here we have taken the real value of capital stock at constant (1981-82) prices as the measure of capital input. Fixed capital represent the depreciated value of fixed assets owned by factory as on the closing day of the accounting year. Fixed capital covers all types of assets, new or used or own constructed, deployed for production, transportation, living or recreational facilities, hospitals, schools etc. for factory personnel. It includes the fixed assets of the head office allocable to the factory and also the full value of assets taken on hire purchase basis (whether fully paid or not) excluding interest element. It excludes intengible assets and assets solely used for post manufacturing activities. The case for inclusion of investment in labour welfare (like living and recreational facilities, hospitals etc.) in capital stock may not be particularly convincing. Probably, these expenses should be treated as investment in durable consumer goods. But we did not have sufficiently disaggregated data to adjust for them. Deflator for fixed capital stock is obtained from data on Gross Fixed Capital Formation (GFCF) at current and constant prices, for different years. Data for the above purpose are obtained from the various issues of Annual Survey of Industries and National Accounts Statistics published by the Central Statistical Organisation.

NOTES

1. An interesting discussion in this connection can be found in Margit and Singh, 1995.

2. The concept seems to have its origin in Tinbergen (1942) but brought to the notice in English language literature on the subject much later by Valavanis-Vail (1955).
3. While the above criticisms are well established in the literature (Nadiri, 1970; Syrquin 1984) their implications for the methodology particularly with respect to an underdeveloped economy like India is important here.
4. This point may be relevant when we compare TFPG of sub-periods in Chapters 3 and 4.
5. The problem arises because we have computed growth rates identically for Solow and Trans-log measures.
6. This is so because we have measured the growth rates in the two cases in the same way though this is not the normal (or, probably, proper) practice. Our objective is to focus on the differences in the indices caused by the differences in the treatment of factor shares.
7. With regard to the problem of identification in the context of the estimation of the production function we should mention that it has been shown (Zellner and others, 1966; Hodges, 1969) for Cobb-Douglas and CES production functions that under some very plausible assumptions the problem does not exist. The assumptions involve the introduction of a random human error in the allocation of resources and the maximisation of *expected* profits.
8. One point in favour of the value added index is that the Central Statistical Organisation uses the double deflation method in arriving at the constant price value added in agriculture and also in some other sectors at least partially. Also, for the manufacturing sector the real value added is arrived at by using the wholesale price index at the aggregate level, not at the two digit or three digit levels of disaggregation.
9. We are particularly vulnerable as we have criticised the assumption of equality of factor shares and factor elasticities. So our use of wage shares of different categories of workers as the weight for the category is an inconsistency which we have indulged in consciously because a better alternative was not immediately clear to us.

3

TFPG: Kendrick, Solow and Trans-Log Measures

I

In this chapter we present our findings regarding total factor productivity growth (TFPG) obtained by three different approaches for two separate measures of output. The approach to the measure of TFPG has been explained in details in the previous chapter. We have computed the Kendrick, Solow and Trans-log indices of total factor productivity (TFP) for nine major two-digit level industries comprising approximately eighty per cent of the total value added in 1982-83, at current prices, in the organised manufacturing sector in India.

Different measures of TFPG have been discussed in the previous chapter. We present here the formulae at the pain of repetition, which form the basis of calculation. Kendrick measure of TFPG for the current period is represented by the following formula:

$$\frac{Y_1/Y_0}{\left(wL_1+rK_1\right)/\left(wL_0+rK_0\right)}-1$$

subscript 1 denotes current period and 0 denotes the previous period. Here w and r are the payments to unit factor inputs capital (K) and labour (L). Y denotes output. Here we have taken a moving base though the index is often computed on the basis of a fixed base.

Solow's measure of TFPG is given by the difference between rate of growth of value added and the rate of growth of total factor inputs as is represented by:

$$G^s = \frac{\dot{A}}{A} = \frac{\dot{Y}}{Y} - \left(\frac{s_k \dot{K}}{K} + \frac{s_l \dot{L}}{L} \right)$$

where s_l and s_k are the wage share and capital share respectively. We checked whether the time series of s_l and s_k show any rising or falling trend. If case is of the existence of such a trend we have used the trend or fitted values of the respective shares in the calculation of the Solow index. Otherwise we have used the arithmetic mean of the whole period for the same. Trans-log index of TFPG is also defined in a similar fashion, the difference being that, instead of using the mean or trend values of the factor shares, two period moving average of the respective factor shares are used for the computation of the index. Thus the difference between the Solow and Trans-log index really arises from the use of a fixed or trend values of shares of inputs (as in Solow index) and the use of the current shares (as in the case of Trans-log index). We have, in fact, eliminated the other source of difference which arises from the difference in the measurement of growth rates. For both the indices we have taken the difference between the successive logarithms as the measure of the rate of growth.

II. ESTIMATES OF TFPG

The period covered by our study is from 1970-71 to 1987-88. In order to facilitate comparison of the estimates we have also computed average annual TFPG for the entire period as well as for two sub-periods 1970-71 to 1980-81 and 1981-82 to 1987-88. Table 3.1 shows the average annual TFPG for all the three alternative measures for the whole as well as the sub-periods as mentioned above. Tables 3A.1 to 3A.9 in the appendix of this chapter show the annual TFP indices (Kendrick, Solow, Trans-log) for the industries that we have taken up for our study. There are two sets of estimates corresponding to two alternative measures of real value added, Y and Z. Thus Table 3.1 presents three alternative measures of TFPG for each of the two measures of value added for nine industries. The measures of real value added, *Y* and *Z*, have been discussed in the last chapter.

Table 3.1: Average Annual TFPG (%)

Indry.	*Variable Y*			*Variable Z*		
	Ken	*Solow*	*Tr.log*	*Ken*	*Solow*	*Tr.log*
1 a	1.86	1.92	1.91	0.80	0.76	0.75
b	1.89	1.42	1.41	0.83	0.23	0.23
c	1.84	2.34	2.33	0.76	1.20	1.20
2 a	2.16	2.13	2.12	1.94	1.58	1.57
b	1.91	2.15	2.07	1.98	2.05	1.97
c	2.79	2.12	2.16	3.26	1.13	1.17
3 a	1.34	1.30	1.26	0.60	0.43	0.38
b	1.80	1.41	1.26	1.44	0.62	0.48
c	0.73	1.19	1.26	-0.49	0.23	0.29
4 a	1.44	1.44	1.36	1.12	1.10	1.02
b	1.01	0.62	0.44	1.68	1.11	0.91
c	2.15	2.49	2.55	0.19	1.10	1.16
5 a	2.58	2.53	2.55	1.40	1.40	1.43
b	3.57	3.42	3.41	2.05	2.18	1.95
c	1.35	1.39	1.43	0.34	0.43	0.47
6 a	1.94	1.92	1.92	1.47	1.43	1.43
b	2.42	2.41	2.39	2.26	2.21	2.21
c	1.25	1.22	1.24	0.37	0.32	0.32
7 a	0.22	0.19	0.19	0.37	0.23	0.26
b	0.77	0.83	0.82	0.95	1.12	1.12
c	-0.70	-0.65	-0.60	-0.72	-0.89	-0.85
8 a	1.21	1.35	1.42	-0.25	-0.24	-0.19
b	1.12	1.17	1.19	-0.05	-0.06	-0.005
c	1.31	1.51	1.65	-0.48	-0.42	-0.33
9 a	0.46	0.16	0.14	0.91	0.83	0.82
b	-2.69	-1.39	-1.41	-1.53	-1.63	-1.65
c	4.36	4.14	4.14	3.88	3.72	3.72

Note: Industry 1: Chemical & Chemical Products. 2: Electricity. 3: Basic Metal & Alloys. 4: Transport Equipment & Parts. 5: Electrical Machinery & Parts. 6: Non-Electrical Machinery. 7: Non-Metallic Mineral Products. 8: Cotton Textiles. 9: Food Products.

Indry = Industry. Ken = Kendrick Measure,

Solow = Solow Measure, Tr. log = Trans-log Measure.

a = 1970-71 to 1987-88, b = 1970-71 to 1980-81

c = 1981-82 to 1987-88.

It is noteworthy that for all the nine industries and for each of the measures of real value added the three measures of TFPG (Kendrick, Solow and Trans-log) give very close results. Thus ranking of industries according to their TFPG is practically independent of the measure of TFPG adopted (rank correlations have been discussed below). However, it should be noted that in general, TFPG is high for variable Y compared to variable Z.[1] All the industries for variable Y show positive TFPG. For variable Z all but Cotton textiles show positive TFPG.

For variable Y, TFPG is highest and marginally above 2.5 per cent per annum for Electrical machinery and parts. It is close to 2 per cent per annum for industries such as Chemical and chemical products, Electricity and Non-electrical machinery. It is between 1.2 to 1.5 per cent per annum for Basic metal and alloys, Transport equipment and parts and Cotton textiles. TFPG is lowest and less than half per cent per annum for Non-metallic mineral products and Food products industry.

The highest TFPG for variable Z occurs for Electricity, which is found to be 1.94 per cent per annum for Kendrick and about 1.6 per cent per annum for Solow and Trans-log indices. It is between 1.2 and 1.5 per cent per annum for Electrical machinery and parts and Non-electrical machineries. TFPG is between 0.75 and 1.2 per cent per annum for Chemical and chemical products, Transport equipment and parts and Food products. It is low and between 0.25 per cent to 0.75 per cent for Basic metal and alloys and Non-metallic mineral products. TFPG turned out to be negative for Cotton textiles industry.

III. TFPG DURING THE 70s AND THE 80s

When we consider TFPG for the two sub-periods of the whole period, as mentioned earlier, it is observed that Kendrick on the one hand and Solow and Trans-log on the other, do not always project the same picture with regard to change in TFPG between the sub-periods. In case of variable Y, Kendrick index for Chemical and chemical products, Electricity and Basic metal and alloys give a different picture *vis-a-vis* Solow and Trans-log indices. For rest of the industries Kendrick index shows the same picture as that of Solow and Trans-log indices. In case of variable Z, we notice that, for Chemical and chemical products, Electricity, Basic metal and alloys and Transport equipment and parts Kendrick posits a different direction of change for the sub-periods *vis-a-vis* Solow and Trans-log measures of TFPG. Rest of the industries show, however, similar directions of change.

It would now be worthwhile to discuss in some greater detail, the three alternative estimates in accordance with the classification made above with respect to the sub-periods. For Chemical and chemical products, for Y variable, though Solow and Trans-log indices show quite significant increase in TFPG in the second half compared to the first, Kendrick index does not support the finding. In fact, it shows a marginal decline in the second half. In case of Electricity we find a rise in TFPG in the second half compared to the first for Kendrick index. Solow and Trans-log indices, however, remains more or less the same over the two sub-periods. Though a sharp fall for Kendrick index is observed for Basic metal and alloys, Solow index shows a marginal decrease and Trans-log index remains the same over the sub-periods for the industry.

For Y variable, a sharp rise in TFPG in the second half compared to the first, for all the indices, is observed for industries Transport equipment and parts and Food products. Completely reverse picture is noticed for Electrical machinery and parts, Non-electrical machinery and Non-metallic mineral products. In fact, Non-metallic mineral products show a change from positive to negative TFPG from the first sub-period to the second sub-period of our study for all the indices. A marginal rise for all the indices in the second half is noticed for Cotton textiles.

So far as Z variable is concerned, Chemical and chemical products show a marginal decline in TFPG for the second half in case of Kendrick index (Table 3.1). Solow and Trans-log indices on the other hand report a sharp rise in the second period compared to the first. In case of Electricity, for the same variable, though Kendrick index shows a sharp increase in the second half the reverse picture is found for Solow and Trans-log indices. Kendrick index of TFPG falls rapidly and turns out to be negative (0.49 per cent per annum), in the second period for Basic metal and alloys. A marginal decline is observed for Solow and Trans-log indices for this industry. The decline is more pronounced in case of the former. For Transport equipment and parts, Kendrick index of TFPG shows a significant decline in the second period. Though Solow index for this industry remains unaltered, Trans-log index shows a marginal increase.

Marked decline in all the estimates of TFPG, for the second period compared to the first, in case of Z variable, is noticed for Electrical machinery and parts, Non-electrical machinery and Non-metallic mineral products. Point to be stressed here is that, Non-metallic mineral product shows negative TFPG in the second half for both Y and Z variables. Negative TFPG for all estimates, for whole as well as for sub-periods is seen for Cotton textiles industry in case of Z variable. A decline in TFPG in the second half compared to the first is also noticed for the same industry. A significant rise in TFPG in the second half is also reported for Food products industry. Significant observation here is that, keeping in line with Y variable, TFPG for all the three estimates for Z variable came out to be negative in the first half.

IV. COMPARISON WITH OTHER STUDIES

It would now be quite interesting to have a comparison, in a broad perspective, between our study and the earlier ones. As pointed out earlier, we have taken up nine major two-digit level industries comprising approximately eighty per cent of the value added in the manufacturing sector in 1982-83. Thus the aggregate of the nine industries represent roughly the overall manufacturing sector. Table 3.2 shows the weighted arithmetic mean of average annual TFPG according to all the three approaches for both Y and Z variables. We present the nine industry average for the whole period as well as the sub-periods.

Table 3.2: Average Annual TFPG for All Industries

Index	*Variable : Y*			*Variable : Z*		
	A	*B*	*C*	*A*	*B*	*C*
Kendrick	1.60	1.45	1.83	1.02	1.17	1.01
Solow	1.57	1.44	1.89	0.91	0.92	0.86
Trans-log	1.56	1.38	1.93	0.89	0.85	0.90

Note: A : 1970-71 to 1987-88. B : 1970-71 to 1980-81. C : 1981-82 to 1987-88.

Source: Based on Table 3.1.

Goldar's (1986) estimates of TFPG for the large scale manufacturing plus electricity sector covering the period 1970-79 are 1.49, 1.53 and 1.35 per cent per annum for Trans-log, Solow and Kendrick indices of TFPG (See Table 3.3). Roughly, our estimates for more or less the same time span turns out to be 1.38, 1.44 and 1.45 per cent per annum for *Y* variable and 0.85, 0.92 and 1.17 per cent per annum in case of *Z* variable. Goldar's estimates for a large period are 1.31, 1.21 and 1.06 per cent per annum. In the study by Ahluwalia (1985) we find that the Trans-log index of TFPG for the registered manufacturing sector over the period 1959-79 to be –0.4 per cent per annum. Trans-log index of TFPG also turned out to be –0.4 per cent per annum for the registered manufacturing sector covering the period 1959-60 to 1985-86 as is shown by Ahluwalia (1991). From the above analysis it seems that, our result has partial resemblance to that of Goldar (1986).

Table 3.3: Comparison of Our Estimate with that of Goldar*

	Kendrick	*Solow*	*Trans-log*
Our Estimate (Y var) (1970-71 to 1980-81)	1.45	1.44	1.38
Goldar's Estimate (1970-79)	1.35	1.53	1.49

*Goldar's coverage of industries is somewhat different.

From Table 3.2, we observe that average annual TFPG for all the indices shows a rise in the second period compared to the first, in case of Y variable, for the manufacturing sector as a whole.

in case of Kendrick and Solow indices. Trans-log index shows a opposite picture. It is further noticed that figures for Y variable for all the cases, are higher than those for the Z variable.

The propounders of turnaround hypothesis in industrial productivity, for the Indian manufacturing sector are of the view that, there is marked rise in TFPG in the eighties compared to the earlier decades. In this connection we may quote Ahluwalia (1991), "There is by now, clear evidence of a turnaround in industrial growth in the eighties. There is, however, still some debate on the timing of the turnaround. Some authors have asserted that the turnaround had begun just after the mid-seventies while others have assigned it primarily to the eighties", Ahluwalia (1991, p.70). In order to explore the turnaround in the growth of productivity and to establish its timing Ahluwalia (1991) has taken up four sub-periods two of which are overlapping. The first half of the sixties is period I. While the time span from the mid-sixties to 1975-76 is designated as period II, a somewhat longer period from 1965-66 to 1979-80 is referred to as period III. The fourth period is from 1980-81 to 1985-86 (first half of the eighties). "There was a qualitative difference in the growth performance during the first half of the eighties. The growth revival was not associated with an acceleration in the growth of factor inputs but was, rather, based on better productivity performance. The experience was different not only from that of the period of the 'drift', i.e., periods II/III but also from that of the 'rapid growth' phase of period I", Ahluwalia (1991, p. 78).

From Table 3.2, we notice moderate increase in TFPG for all the three indices (Kendrick, Solow and Trans-log) in the second period (the eighties) compared to the first in the case of Y variable for the organised manufacturing sector as a whole. In the case of variable Z while Kendrick and Solow indices show a moderate fall in TFPG in the eighties compared to the seventies, Trans-log index registers a moderate rise in the second period. In this respect we may again quote Ahluwalia (1991), "As for productivity performance the first half of the eighties presents an unambiguously better picture. The acceleration in the growth of total factor productivity is recorded by manufacturing and ..... For the manufacturing sector the turnaround is from a negative and negligible growth in total factor productivity of –0.2/–0.3 per cent per annum in periods II and III to a significant 3.4 per cent per annum in the first half of the eighties", Ahluwalia (1991, p.78). Our findings, of course, are rather different. During the seventies TFPG was positive and quite significant and the acceleration in the eighties though significant, nowhere near the magnitude found by Ahluwalia.[2] Thus our estimates for the Y variable, partially supports the turnaround hypothesis, though Z variable does not speak the same.

If we look at the individual industries, instead of talking about the overall manufacturing sector, it is interesting to note that (Table 3.1), important industries (in terms of share in total manufacturing production) like Basic metal and alloys, Electrical machinery and parts, Non-electrical machineries and Non-metallic mineral products, in general, show a sharp decline in TFPG in the second period compared to the first, for all the three indices. Considering fifty-four cases, six for each industry as shown in Table 3.1, we observe that, in more than thirty cases we have a decline in TFPG for the second period (the eighties), compared to the first (the seventies). Hence, the evidence of turnaround is not unequivocal.

V. RANKING OF INDUSTRIES ACCORDING TO TFPG

Table 3.4 presents the ranking of various industries in accordance with the average annual TFPG for various estimates of the same. The rank correlation coefficients between various indices as well as for variables *Y* and *Z* are shown in Table 3.5. From Table 3.5, we notice that the rank correlation coefficient between Kendrick and Trans-log, Solow and Trans-log and Kendrick and Solow indices of TFPG, for *Y* variable, are respectively 0.9333, 0.9750 and 0.9583. The estimates for the *Z* variable are 0.9917, 0.9917 and 1 respectively. Thus, it seems that the ranking of industries according to various estimates (Kendrick, Solow and Trans-log) of TFPG are almost the same for each of the value added indices used. It is also of interest to note the rank correlation coefficient between Kendrick index of TFPG for *Y* variable and the same index for *Z* variable. Similarly the cases for Solow and Trans-log indices of TFPG are also of interest. The rank correlation coefficients are 0.7833, 0.6667

Table 3.4: Industry Ranks for Kendrick, Solow and Trans-log Indices

Indry.	*Variable : Y*			*Variable : Z*		
	Ken	*Solow*	*Tr. Log*	*Ken*	*Solow*	*Tr. log*
1.	4	3.5	4	6	6	6
2.	2	2	2	1	1	1
3.	6	7	7	7	7	7
4.	5	5	6	4	4	4
5.	1	1	1	3	3	2.5
6.	3	3.5	3	2	2	2.5
7.	9	8	8	8	8	8
8.	7	6	5	9	9	9
9.	8	9	9	5	5	5

Notes: Industry 1: Chemical & Chemical Products. 2: Electricity. 3 : Basic Metal & Alloys. 4: Transport Equipment & Parts. 5: Electrical Machinery & Parts. 6: Non-Electrical Machinery. 7: Non-Metallic Mineral Products. 8: Cotton Textiles. 9: Food Products. Indry. = Industry, Ken = Kendrick measure, Solow = Solow measure, Tr. log = Trans-log measure.

Table 3.5: Rank Correlation Coefficients

Different Indices for Variable Y	
Kendrick Vs Solow	0.9583
Kendrick Vs Trans-log	0.9333
Solow Vs Trans-log	0.9750
Different Indices for Variable Z	
Kendrick Vs Solow	1.0000
Kendrick Vs Trans-log	0.9917
Solow Vs Trans-log	0.9917
Same Index : Vaiable Y Vs Variable Z	
Kendrick (Y) Vs Kendrick (Z)	0.7833
Solow (Y) Vs Solow (Z)	.0.6667
Trans-log (Y) Vs Trans-log (Z)	0.6333

and 0.6333 respectively. Hence, it may be concluded that the ranking based on the average annual TFPG for various indices, does in fact, to a certain extent depend on the measurement of the value added index, though not so much on which of the three indices of TFPG (Kendrick, Solow, Trans-log) is used. This highlights the importance of proper measurement of real value added.

NOTES

1. Y-measure of real value added shows a higher rate of growth than the Z-measure. This is reflected in TFPG.
2. The next chapter presents results from regression analysis.

Appendix to Chapter 3

Table 3A.1: Total Factor Productivity Indices. Kendrick, Solow, Trans-log Measures

Chemical and Chemical Products

Year	*Variable : Y*			*Variable : Z*		
	Ken	*Solow*	*Tr. Log*	*Ken*	*Solow*	*Tr. Log*
1973-74	1.000	1.000	1.000	1.000	1.000	1.000
1974-75	1.022	1.021	1.021	1.073	1.067	1.067
1975-76	1.009	1.008	1.008	1.049	1.042	1.042
1976-77	1.059	1.056	1.056	1.062	1.054	1.054
1977-78	1.067	1.064	1.064	1.039	1.030	1.030
1978-79	1.104	1.102	1.102	1.104	1.092	1.092
1979-80	1.092	1.088	1.088	1.037	1.015	1.015
1981-82	1.144	1.139	1.139	1.074	1.051	1.051
1982-83	1.209	1.198	1.196	1.123	1.094	1.093
1983-84	1.193	1.188	1.186	1.135	1.111	1.110
1984-85	1.243	1.234	1.232	1.124	1.098	1.096
1985-86	1.240	1.235	1.234	1.107	1.084	1.083
1986-87	1.264	1.266	1.265	1.091	1.071	1.071
1987-88	1.279	1.280	1.279	1.127	1.105	1.104

Table 3A.2: Total Factor Productivity Indices. Kendrick, Solow, Trans-Log Measures

Electricity

Year	*Variable : Y*			*Variable : Z*		
	Ken	*Solow*	*Tr. Log*	*Ken*	*Solow*	*Tr. Log*
1973-74	1.000	1.000	1.000	1.000	1.000	1.000
1974-75	1.059	1.058	1.055	1.007	1.007	1.004
1975-76	1.143	1.140	1.133	1.203	1.180	1.172
1976-77	1.147	1.143	1.136	1.186	1.160	1.153
1977-78	1.089	1.079	1.073	1.169	1.143	1.136
1978-79	1.108	1.099	1.091	1.303	1.266	1.258
1979-80	1.109	1.099	1.094	1.225	1.180	1.175
1980-81	1.172	1.160	1.154	1.197	1.150	1.145
1981-82	1.251	1.237	1.230	1.419	1.338	1.331
1982-83	1.247	1.232	1.224	1.371	1.290	1.281
1983-84	1.322	1.305	1.297	1.520	1.421	1.412
1984-85	1.253	1.229	1.221	1.303	1.168	1.161
1985-86	1.307	1.283	1.279	1.378	1.235	1.231
1986-87	1.393	1.365	1.361	1.510	1.347	1.344
1987-88	1.370	1.343	1.341	1.401	1.239	1.237

Note: Ken = Kendrick Measure, Solow = Solow Measure, Tr. log = Trans-log Measure

Table 3A.3: Total Factor Productivity Indices. Kendrick, Solow, Trans-log Measures

Basic Metal and Alloys

Year	*Variable : Y*			*Variable : Z*		
	Ken	*Solow*	*Tr. Log*	*Ken*	*Solow*	*Tr. Log*
1973-74	1.000	1.000	1.000	1.000	1.000	1.000
1974-75	1.089	1.090	1.089	1.131	1.123	1.122
1975-76	1.033	1.018	1.010	1.074	1.051	1.044
1976-77	1.048	1.034	1.023	1.088	1.065	1.055
1977-78	1.055	1.041	1.030	1.017	0.986	0.976
1978-79	1.103	1.087	1076	1.099	1.061	1.052
1979-80	1.099	1.083	1.071	1.066	1.027	1.017
1980-81	1.119	1.103	1.091	1.086	1.046	1.035
1981-82	1.163	1.146	1.132	1.148	1.103	1.091
1982-83	1.199	1.181	1.166	1.116	1.071	1.058
1983-84	1.134	1.111	1.096	1.114	1.070	1.056
1984-85	1.142	1.120	1.107	1.061	1.014	1.003
1985-86	1.176	1.154	1.144	1.174	1.113	1.104
1986-87	1.220	1.196	1.184	1.104	1.039	1.029
1987-88	1.219	1.198	1.191	1.128	1.064	1.057

Table 3A.4: Total Factor Productivity Indices. Kendrick, Solow, Trans-Log Measures

Transport Equipment and Parts

Year	*Variable : Y*			*Variable : Z*		
	Ken	*Solow*	*Tr. Log*	*Ken*	*Solow*	*Tr. Log*
1973-74	1.000	1.000	1.000	1.000	1.000	1.000
1974-75	0.993	0.998	0.997	1.049	1.054	1.053
1975-76	1.014	1.017	1.016	1.108	1.109	1.108
1976-77	1.068	1.064	1.060	1.141	1.135	1.130
1977-78	1.052	1.048	1.043	1.111	1.104	1.099
1978-79	0.979	0.975	0.954	1.081	1.083	1.057
1979-80	0.968	0.954	0.939	1.055	1.045	1.027
1980-81	1.002	0.986	0.971	1.086	1.074	1.057
1981-82	1.041	1.024	1.009	1.155	1.139	1.121
1982-83	1.069	1.051	1.036	1.195	1.178	1.159
1983-84	1.083	1.066	1.050	1.187	1.170	1.152
1984-85	1.090	1.074	1.059	1.166	1.151	1.133
1985-86	1.120	1.105	1.091	1.158	1.145	1.129
1986-87	1.162	1.147	1.133	1.212	1.199	1.183
1987-88	1.184	1.173	1.159	1.172	1.160	1.146

Table 3A.5: Total Factor Productivity Indices. Kendrick, Solow, Trans-log Measures

Electrical Machinery and Parts

Year	*Variable : Y*			*Variable : Z*		
	Ken	*Solow*	*Tr. Log*	*Ken*	*Solow*	*Tr. Log*
1973-74	1.000	1.000	1.000	1.000	1.000	1.000
1974-75	0.957	0.952	0.952	1.005	1.005	1.005
1975-76	1.008	1.002	1.002	1.080	1.076	1.077
1976-77	1.063	1.056	1.056	1.061	1.056	1.056
1977-78	1.075	1.068	1.068	1.058	1.052	1.052
1978-79	1.097	1.091	1.091	1.081	1.076	1.076
1979-80	1.114	1.109	1.111	1.080	1.076	1.078
1980-81	1.174	1.168	1.169	1.101	1.097	1.098
1981-82	1.192	1.187	1.189	1.100	1.097	1.098
1982-83	1.230	1.224	1.225	1.145	1.139	1.140
1983-84	1.193	1.183	1.184	1.131	1.124	1.125
1984-85	1.217	1.207	1.208	1.189	1.181	1.182
1985-86	1.243	1.234	1.235	1.114	1.095	1.097
1986-87	1.273	1.264	1.268	1.132	1.114	1.117
1987-88	1.293	1.286	1.292	1.148	1.131	1.136

Table 3A.6: Total Factor Productivity Indices. Kendrick, Solow Trans-log Measures

Non-Electrical Machinery

Year	*Variable : Y*			*Variable : Z*		
	Ken	*Solow*	*Tr. Log*	*Ken*	*Solow*	*Tr. Log*
1973-74	1.000	1.000	1.000	1.000	1.000	1.000
1974-75	1.054	1.053	1.053	1.074	1.070	1.070
1975-76	1.041	1.039	1.038	1.110	1.106	1.106
1976-77	1.096	1.093	1.091	1.154	1.149	1.147
1977-78	1.081	1.076	1.075	1.105	1.096	1.095
1978-79	1.124	1.119	1.119	1.153	1.143	1.143
1979-80	1.113	1.109	1.110	1.121	1.110	1.111
1980-81	1.175	1.168	1.169	1.176	1.163	1.164
1981-82	1.170	1.164	1.165	1.176	1.164	1.165
1982-83	1.190	1.184	1.185	1.194	1.181	1.182
1983-84	1.168	1.159	1.163	1.182	1.168	1.172
1984-85	1.218	1.208	1.212	1.264	1.245	1.250
1985-86	1.190	1.182	1.186	1.215	1.196	1.201
1986-87	1.253	1.240	1.244	1.223	1.202	1.205
1987-88	1.287	1.274	1.277	1.212	1.190	1.193

Table 3A.7: Total Factor Productivity Indices. Kendrick, Solow, Trans-Log Measures

Non-Metallic Mineral Products

Year	*Variable : Y*			*Variable : Z*		
	Ken	*Solow*	*Tr. Log*	*Ken*	*Solow*	*Tr. Log*
1973-74	1.000	1.000	1.000	1.000	1.000	1.000
1974-75	1.005	1.006	1.002	1.061	1.060	1.055
1975-76	1.023	1.024	1.019	1.166	1.159	1.154
1976-77	1.057	1.057	1.052	1.168	1.159	1.154
1977-78	1.088	1.089	1.085	1.232	1.222	1.217
1978-79	1.037	1.036	1.033	1.186	1.178	1.174
1979-80	1.049	1.047	1.043	1.188	1.179	1.175
1980-81	1.051	1.043	1.042	1.183	1.166	1.165
1981-82	1.046	1.036	1.038	1.169	1.149	1.152
1982-83	1.048	1.037	1.040	1.290	1.258	1.264
1983-84	0.993	0.974	0.979	1.241	1.204	1.211
1984-85	1.048	1.026	1.032	1.321	1.279	1.287
1985-86	1.031	1.012	1.017	1.254	1.213	1.220
1986-87	1.011	0.997	1.001	1.130	1.083	1.087
1987-88	1.008	0.997	0.999	1.136	1.092	1.096

Table 3A.8: Total Factor Productivity Indices. Kendrick, Solow, Trans-log Measures

Cotton Textiles

Year	*Variable : Y*			*Variable : Z*		
	Ken	*Solow*	*Tr. Log*	*Ken*	*Solow*	*Tr. Log*
1973-74	1.000	1.000	1.000	1.000	1.000	1.000
1974-75	1.021	1.029	1.031	0.985	0.989	0.990
1975-76	1.049	1.058	1.059	0.954	0.957	0.957
1976-77	1.063	1.069	1.074	0.956	0.957	0.959
1977-78	1.071	1.075	1.081	0.974	0.973	0.976
1978-79	1.095	1.098	1.104	1.019	1.013	1.017
1979-80	1.073	1.076	1.084	1.016	1.011	1.015
1980-81	1.082	1.085	1.086	1.003	0.998	0.998
1981-82	1.084	1.087	1.087	0.976	0.969	0.969
1982-83	1.080	1.085	1.088	0.946	0.938	0.939
1983-84	1.103	1.114	1.121	0.984	0.976	0.980
1984-85	1.126	1.143	1.153	0.964	0.957	0.963
1985-86	1.157	1.180	1.192	0.974	0.970	0.976
1986-87	1.139	1.157	1.169	0.985	0.980	0.986
1987-88	1.189	1.206	1.219	0.977	0.971	0.977

Table 3A.9: Total Factor Productivity Indices. Kendrick, Solow, Trans-log Measures

Food Products

Year	*Variable : Y*			*Variable : Z*		
	Ken	*Solow*	*Tr. Log*	*Ken*	*Solow*	*Tr. Log*
1973-74	1.000	1.000	1.000	1.000	1.000	1.000
1974-75	1.024	1.025	1.029	1.012	1.013	1.017
1975-76	1.052	1.056	1.061	1.016	1.021	1.026
1976-77	1.025	1.027	1.031	1.023	1.027	1.031
1977-78	1.064	1.062	1.064	1.025	1.026	1.027
1978-79	1.210	1.190	1.191	1.018	1.017	1.018
1979-80	1.089	1.054	1.055	1.007	1.007	1.007
1980-81	0.949	0.896	0.894	0.941	0.937	0.935
1981-82	1.061	0.993	0.990	1.018	1.010	1.007
1982-83	1.212	1.115	1.113	1.111	1.093	1.092
1983-84	1.200	1.103	1.101	1.247	1.214	1.212
1984-85	1.207	1.110	1.108	1.213	1.178	1.177
1985-86	1.260	1.157	1.155	1.239	1.204	1.202
1986-87	1.260	1.161	1.158	1.240	1.209	1.206
1987-88	1.293	1.190	1.187	1.241	1.209	1.207

Average Annual TFPG (Var. Y) Kendrick, Solow, Trans-log

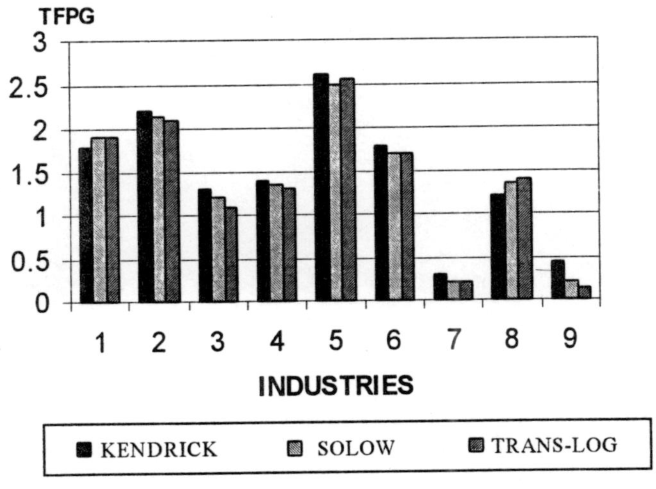

Average Annual TFPG (Var. Z)
Kendrick, Solow, Trans-log

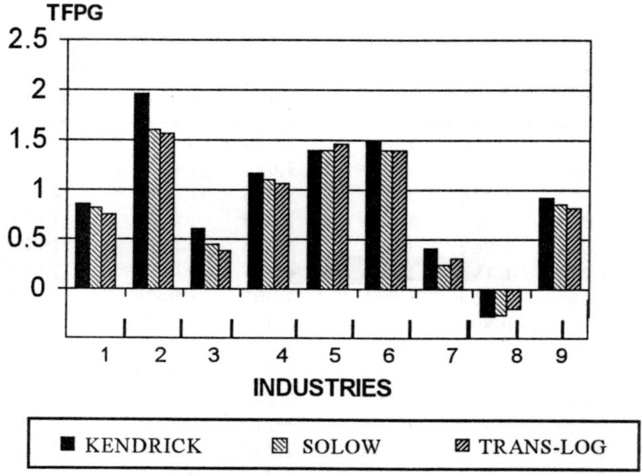

4

TFPG: Production Function Approach

I

In this chapter we discuss the estimation of the total factor productivity through the estimation of the production function. As we have discussed in chapter 2, the production function has been obtained through a process of backward elimination starting from the general trans-log production function. The final forms of the production function that have been used to obtain the TFPG have passed a three-fold test of observational robustness, joint insignificance of the coefficients (of the general form of the trans-log production function) that have been assumed to be zero for the final forms of the production function used in our estimates of TFPG and a positive contribution of inputs to the growth of output. The general form of the trans-log production function (including a slope dummy) is:

$$\log Y = \alpha_0 + \alpha Dt + \alpha_1 \log K + \alpha_2 \log L + \alpha_3 T + \frac{1}{2}(\beta_{11} \log^2 K + \beta_{22} \log^2 L + \beta_{33} T^2) + \beta_{12} \log K \log L + \beta_{13} \log K.T + \beta_{23} \log L.T$$

The final forms of the production function, as mentioned above, do not contain all the coefficients of the general form. Normally, they contain five to seven terms or coefficients. Further, the final form contains as its arguments all the variables—capital, labour and time.

Here we present the estimates of production function for nine major industries of the organised manufacturing sector of the Indian economy for the period 1970-71 to 1987-88 and estimates of total factor productivity growth obtained from these production functions. All the regression results that pass the above mentioned tests have been presented in the Tables 4A.1 to 4A.9 in the appendix of this chapter. As already discussed, we have two measures of output, Y and Z. Thus for each industry we have two sets of results.

A slope dummy (in the form of 'dummy · time') has been included in the regression exercise to account for shift in the TFPG. It should be mentioned here that we have tried with alternative dummy variables (such as D8, D9, D10 etc.) in our regression analysis. D8 takes the value zero upto seventh observation and one from eighth observation onwards. D9, D10 etc. are also defined similarly.

The existence of high degree of multicollinearity may possibly have lent some uncertainty to our analysis. We know that high degree of multicollinearity makes the variance of coefficients high and thus makes the t-statistic an unreliable guide to the significance of the individual parameters. Fortunately, we had very low standard error of estimates. This offsets the effect of high variance to some extent. Further, the three-fold test mentioned above should go in some way in giving credibility to our results.

Here we would like to discuss one point in some detail. Since in dropping terms of the trans-log production function we have been guided by the t-test on individual parameters, as an additional check we have undertaken F-test of significance of the joint exclusion of variables from the production function. We may mention that the F-test takes into account the effect of intercorrelations and it often gives conflicting signals *vis-a-vis* t-test for individual parameters, when multicollinearity is strong. We have used the F-statistic:

$$F_{\mathrm{q,n-k}} = \frac{R_{\mathrm{g}}^2 - R_{\mathrm{c}}^2}{1 - R_{\mathrm{g}}^2} \cdot \frac{n-k}{q}$$

(Where n, k and q are respectively the number of observations, the number of coefficients in the general form of the production function and number of independent linear restrictions, i.e., the number of coefficients assumed zero in the present case).

Here R^2_g is the R^2 value for the general case regression, R^2_c is the R^2 value for the final form regression, $(n–k)$ and $(n–k+q)$ are the degrees of freedom for the general case and the final form regression respectively. Tables 4.1 and 4.1′ shows the results of F-test for all our good fit regressions presented in Tables 4A.1 to 4A.9. The test shows that the dropped terms were not significant jointly so far as the data at hand are concerned. This along with the fact that the t-statistics are highly significant for all the coefficients of the final form of our production functions and that these final forms are observationally robust, makes out estimates interesting.

Table 4.1: F-Test of Joint Restrictions on Parameters (Variable Y)

Indry.	R^2_c	$df = n–k+q$	R^2_g	$df = n-k$	$\$Fq,\ n-k$
1.i	0.9996	7	0.99966	3	0.20
1.ii	0.9996	7	0.99966	3	0.20
1.iii	0.9996	7	0.99966	3	0.20
1.iv	0.9996	7	0.99966	3	0.20
1.v	0.9932	11	0.99966	3	6.19
2.i	0.988	11	0.995	4	0.8
2.ii	0.966	12	0.995	4	2.9
3.i	0.982	11	0.998	4	4.57
3.ii	0.982	11	0.988	4	4.57
4.i	0.9943	12	0.9985	6	2.80
4.ii	0.9869	14	0.9985	6	5.30
5.i	0.9889	15	0.9907	6	0.129
5.ii	0.9840	14	0.9907	6	0.540
6.i	0.994	13	0.997	6	0.857
6.ii	0.995	12	0.997	6	0.667
7.i	0.994	12	0.997	6	1.00
7.ii	0.993	12	0.997	6	1.33
7.iii	0.993	12	0.997	6	1.33
7.iv	0.993	13	0.997	6	1.143
7.v	0.988	14	0.997	6	2.25
8.i	0.978	9	0.992	4	1.40
8.ii	0.924	12	0.992	4	4.25
9.i	0.928	9	0.978	5	2.84

$\$\ F_{q,\,n-k} = (n-k) \times (R^2_g - R^2_c)/q \times (1 - R^2_g)$

Notes: Indry: Industry 1: Chemical & Chemical Products. 2: Electricity. 3. Basic Metal & Alloys. 4: Transport Equipment & Parts. 5: Electrical Machinery & Parts. 6: Non-Electrical Machinery. 7: Non-Metallic Mineral Products. 8: Cotton Textiles. 9: Food Products.

Roman numerals represent regressions for the same industry ranked according to the value of R^2.

Table 4.1′ : F-Test of Joint Restrictions on Parameters (Variable Z)

Indry.	R^2_c	$df=n-k+q$	R^2_g	$df=n-k$	$\$Fq,n-k$
1.	0.945	10	0.975	3	0.514
2.	0.950	11	0.976	4	0.619
3.i	0.937	9	0.967	4	0.727
3.ii	0.912	10	0.967	4	1.11
4.	0.991	8	0.992	6	0.375
5.	0.982	11	0.993	6	1.89
6.i	0.985	13	0.994	6	1.29
6.ii	0.983	13	0.994	6	1.57
7.	0.974	12	0.993	6	2.71
8.	0.920	8	0.972	4	1.86
9.	0.879	12	0.981	4	2.68

$\$ F_{q,n-k} = (n-k) \times (R^2_g - R^2_c)/q \times (1 - R^2_g)$

Notes: Indry: Industry 1: Chemical & Chemical Products. 2: Electricity. 3: Basic Metal & Alloys, 4: Transport Equipment & Parts. 5: Electrical Machinery & Parts. 6: Non-Electrical Machinery. 7: Non-Metallic Mineral products. 8: Cotton Textiles. 9: Food products.

Roman numerals represent regressions for the same industry ranked according to the value of R^2.

The use of trans-log production function gives us some advantage. Each variable L, K and T is represented through four terms in the production function. While this is one cause for high multicollinearity, this also makes easier the dropping of variables selectively from the regression. It may be noted that dropping of a few terms may not leave the resulting form of the production function devoid of the influence of the variables K, L or T, but in the process the severity of the influence of multicollinearity may be avoided substantially. In Tables 4A.1 to 4A.9 we present the regression results representing the estimated production functions. As mentioned above, these regressions are observationally robust, they have with all the coefficients statistically significant and, further, all the variables K, L and T are represented in them.

II. TFPG ESTIMATES FROM PRODUCTION FUNCTIONS

The period covered by our study is from 1970-71 to 1987-88. In order to facilitate comparison of the performance during the 70s with that during the 80s we have computed average annual TFPG for the entire as well as for the two sub-periods 1970-71 to 1980-81 and 1981-82 to 1987-88. Table 4.2 shows the average annual TFPG for the whole as well as sub-periods for all the nine two-digit level industries for the Y variable. Similarly, Table 4.3 shows the average annual TFPG, for the whole as well as sub-periods, computed from regression analysis, for all the nine industries in case of Z variable.

From Table 4.2, we notice that there are altogether five regressions passing all the four stages for Chemical and chemical products and Non-metallic mineral products. For all other industries except Food products we have two good fit regressions. For Food products we have only one regression. Regression 1, has been chosen from those passing the tests mentioned above on the basis of the highest value of R^2 for all the nine industries.

In fact, the difference between R^2 values for all the alternative results presented in Tables 4.11 to 4.19 is very small in most cases. For Chemical and chemical products and Non-metallic mineral products, we notice that all the five regressions give very close estimates of average annual TFPG for the whole period. This observation is true for four other industries but for the three remaining industries, namely, Electricity, Electrical machineries and parts and Cotton textiles, estimates of TFPG vary widely for the alternative estimates of the production function. So, there is some ambiguity with respect to the three industries so far as the Y-measure of output is concerned.

From Table 4.3 we observe that for the Z variable Basic metal and alloy and Non-electrical machinery we have two regressions each giving us close TFPG results. Rest of the industries show only one regression passing the tests noted above. So, results for the Z variable are unambiguous. It is very significant that for all the three industries just mentioned showing diverse TFPG estimates for the Y variable, the estimates for the Z variable are very much closer to those obtained from regression 1 (with higher R^2) compared to the estimates given by regression 2 for the Y variable. This closeness, apart from higher R^2, gives us the basis to emphasize the estimates from regression 1 in our subsequent analysis. In the following discussion, unless otherwise mentioned, our analysis would be centred around the best regression (regression 1) for both the variables Y and Z of all the nine industries.

Table 4.2: Average Annual TFPG: Production Function Approach: (Variable Y)(%)

		Reg.1	*Reg.2*	*Reg.3*	*Reg.4*	*Reg.5*
Industry: 1	a	3.31	3.26	3.33	3.30	3.05
	b	2.70	2.75	3.39	3.35	3.50
	c	3.91	3.79	3.27	3.25	2.62
Industry:2	a	3.53	0.65			
	b	3.40	0.63			
	c	3.66	0.67			
Industry:3	a	2.93	2.90			
	b	3.04	3.01			
	c	2.81	2.77			
Industry: 4	a	2.34	2.23			
	b	1.81	2.12			
	c	3.11	2.39			
Industry: 5	a	2.08	0.42			
	b	2.04	0.27			
	c	2.17	0.63			
Industry: 6	a	2.41	2.47			
	b	2.35	2.43			
	c	2.49	2.52			
Industry: 7	a	1.77	1.74	1.63	1.57	1.26
	b	1.78	1.74	1.71	1.62	1.22
	c	1.73	1.74	1.52	1.52	1.32
Industry: 8	a	0.03	1.16			
	b	1.10	0.89			
	c	−1.17	1.47			
Industry: 9	a	0.64				
	b	−1.51				
	c	3.47				

Notes: Industry numbers explained in Table 4.1.

a: 1970-71 to 1987-88. b: 1970-71 to 1980-81. c: 1981-82 to 1987-88. Reg. = Regression. Regressions for the same industry have been ranked according to the value of R^2.

For variable Y, in case of Chemical and chemical products, TFPG for the whole period, in general is close for all the five regressions. It ranges from 3.05 to 3.33 per cent per annum as is seen from Table 4.2. It is noticed that for Basic metal and alloy, Transport equipment and parts and Non-Electrical machinery, best and the second best regression provide us very close TFPG over the whole period. Electricity, Electrical machinery and parts and Cotton textiles show wide disparity for the same. Non-metallic mineral products, in general, show close results for the five good fit regressions that is presented in Table. 4.2. Thus for six out of nine industries the TFPG estimates corresponding to different regressions (or underlying production functions) are very close. For one industry there is only one regression. But for two industries TFPG estimates vary substantially for the two regressions in each case.

Table 4.3: Average Annual TFPG: Production Function Approach: (variable Z)(%)

		Reg. 1	*Reg.2*
Industry: 1	a	1.80	
	b	1.74	
	c	1.87	
Industry: 2	a	3.06	
	b	4.31	
	c	1.65	
Industry: 3	a	1.72	1.85
	b	2.58	2.88
	c	0.73	0.66
Industry: 4	a	3.54	
	b	2.76	
	c	4.66	
Industry: 5	a	1.67	
	b	2.66	
	c	0.26	
Industry: 6	a	2.56	2.28
	b	2.95	3.82
	c	2.01	0.11
Industry: 7	a	0.98	
	b	1.56	
	c	0.18	
Industry: 8	a	–0.28	
	b	–0.09	
	c	–0.48	
Industry: 9	a	0.34	
	b	0.06	
	c	0.07	

Notes: Notations as in Table 4.2.

For variable Y, TFPG is highest and marginally above 3.5 per cent per annum for Electricity (for regression 1). Industry Electricity is followed by Chemical and chemical products, with TFPG 3.31 per cent per annum. TFPG is between 2 to 3 per cent per annum for Basic metal and alloy, Non-electrical machinery, Transport equipment and parts and Electrical machinery (for regression 1). It is marginally above 1.75 per cent per annum for Non-metallic mineral products. TFPG is low and less than 0.75 per cent per annum for Food products and Cotton textiles. It is lowest for Cotton textiles.

For variable Z, we observe that only two industries, Basic metal and alloy and Non-electrical machinery turns up with two regressions. The rest shows only one regression. In case of Basic metal and alloy, though TFPG varies from 1.72 to 1.85 per cent per annum, the results seem to be close. Similar is the picture for Non-electrical machinery. Thus our results for the Z variable are quite unambiguous.

Highest TFPG (marginally above 3.5 per cent) for variable Z is reported for Transport equipment and parts. It is followed by Electricity, whose TFPG is marginally above 3 per cent per annum. (It may be noted that this result is very close to that obtained from regression 1, for the Y variable.) TFPG is slightly above 2.5 per cent per annum for Non-electrical machinery. It is between 1.5 to 2 per cent per annum for Chemical and chemical products, Basic metal and alloy and Electrical machinery. TFPG is less than one per cent per annum for Non-metallic mineral products, Cotton textiles and Food products. It turns out to be negative for cotton textiles.

III. INDUSTRY RANKS ACCORDING TO TFPG

Table 4.4 presents the ranking of various industries in accordance with TFPG for the best regression in case of both the variables Y and Z. Looking at Table 4.4 we see that the group of top five industries ranked according to TFPG for variables Y and Z are identical. This group consists of industries Chemical and chemical products, Electricity, Basic metal and alloy, Transport equipment and parts and Non-electrical machinery. Further, what is more striking, industries with ranks from 6 to 9 according to TFPG for both Y and Z estimates of output are identical.

Table 4.4: Industry Ranking according to TFPG (Variables Y and Z)

Industry	*Variable Y*	*Variable Z*
Electricity	1	2
Chemical & Chemical Products	2	4
Basic Metal & Alloys	3	5
Non-Electrical Machinery	4	3
Transport Equipment & Parts	5	1
Electrical Machinery & Parts	6	6
Non-Metallic Mineral Products	7	7
Food Products	8	8
Cotton Textiles	9	9
Rank Correlation Coefficient = 0.7833		

The rank correlation coefficient for the two rankings of industries, according to TFPG for variables Y and Z comes out to be 0.7833. Thus, it may be commented that the ranking of industries based on average annual TFPG obtained from the estimation of production function are broadly similar for Y and Z variables. This is true in spite of the fact that the measures Y and Z vary a great deal. The growth of Y is higher than that of Z and this is reflected in higher TFPG estimates for Y variable compared to the Z variable.

While the similarity of ranking is satisfying so far as our analysis is concerned, the differences are also not to be ignored. Rankings for the group of top (with respect to TFPG) five industries are not identical and, as just mentioned, the estimates of TFPG are different. Thus, clearly, the measures do in fact, to a certain extent depend on the measurement of the value added index. As in the case of other measures of TFPG discussed in Chapter 3, this also highlights the significance of proper measurement of real value added.

IV. TFPG DURING THE 70s AND THE 80s

When we consider TFPG for the two sub-periods of the whole period, 1970-71 to 1980-81 and 1981-82 to 1987-88, it is noticed that a more or less similar picture is projected for the first and second regressions for variable Y with regard to change in TFPG between the sub-periods (Table 4.2). The only exception is Cotton textiles for variable Y, where the first regression shows a marked fall in TFPG (in fact TFPG turns out to be negative) in the second period compared to the first and a opposite picture is reported for the second regression. Table 4.5 presents the change in TFPG in the second sub-period compared to the first for both the first and the second regressions for variables Y and Z with respect to the nine industries that we have taken up for study. So far our comparison in case of best regression between variables Y and Z is concerned, it is noticed that industries, Chemical and chemical products, Basic metal and alloy, Transport equipment and parts, Non-metallic mineral products, Cotton textiles and Food products show a more or less similar trend with respect to the change in TFPG in the second period compared to the first. For the remaining three industries picture obtained from the two variables are different.

Table 4.5: Change in TFPG in the 80s Compared to the 70s@

Industry		*Variable Y*	*Variable Z*	*Share* *
1	a	Rises.	Rises marginally.	12.3%
	b	Rises.	—	
2	a	Rises marginally.	Falls sharply.	14.5%
	b	Rises marginally.	—	
3	a	Falls.	Falls.	10.8%
	b	Falls.	Falls.	
4	a	Rises.	Rises.	7.9%
	b	Rises marginally.	—	
5	a	Rises marginally.	Falls	7.2%
	b	Rises marginally.	—	
6	a	Rises marginally.	Falls.	7.1%
	b	Rises marginally.	Falls	
7	a	Falls marginally.	Falls	4.4%
	b	Remains the same.	—	
8	a	Falls.	Falls.	7.0%
	b	Rises.	—	
9.	a	Rises.	Remains the same	7.1%
	b	—	—	

Notes: Industry numbers as in earlier tables.
@ :Based on tables 4.2 and 4.3.
a : Refers to the first regression.
b : Refers to the second regression.
* : Industry share in total manufacturing production based on data for the year 1982-83 at current prices.

It would now be worthwhile to discuss in some greater detail, the two alternative estimates of TFPG (for variables Y and Z) for the best regression with the classification made above with respect to the sub-periods. While a sharp rise in TFPG in the second half compared to the first is reported in case of Y variable for Chemical and chemical products, Z variable shows a marginal increase for the same. Both Y and Z in case of Transport equipment and parts shows marked rise in TFPG in the second half compared to the first. In case of Basic metal and alloy, while Y variable presents a marginal decline, Z variable shows a pronounced fall in TFPG for the second period in contrast to the first. Though TFPG in the second sub-period remains more or less the same (a slight fall), in the second half in respect to the first, for variable Y, Z variable registers a marked fall in case of Non-metallic mineral products. For cotton textiles, TFPG shows a marked decline and turned out to be significantly negative in the second sub-period in case of Y variable. For this industry TFPG though negative in the first half registers a moderate decline in the second half. In case of Food products, though TFPG was negative in the first half, turned out to be strongly positive for variable Y. Variable Z for this industry shows practically no change in TFPG over the sub-periods.

While TFPG in the second period shows marginal increase in case of variable Y for Electricity, Z variable registers a drastic fall. Similar picture is also observed for Electrical machinery and parts. Though a marginal increase in TFPG for the second sub-period in comparison to the first is noted for variable Y in case of Non-electrical machinery, Z variable reports a moderate decline for the same.

Thus while there is rather a broad similarity as regards the direction of change whether measured for the Y or the Z variable, the similarity is much less pronounced as regards the magnitude of change. Thus the picture presented by the two variables Y and Z are similar to a great extent so far as we confine ourselves to the broad trends or rankings. The more we enter into greater details, the less is the comparability. We would like to add here that this is true not only for our estimates via production function but more or less so also for other measures of TFPG presented in Chapter 3.

V. COMPARISON WITH OTHERS' FINDINGS

It would be of much interest to have some sort of a comparison, in a broad sense, between our study and the previous ones. As is pointed out in the previous chapter, we would consider the aggregate of nine industries to represent roughly the overall manufacturing sector.[1] Table 4.6 shows the weighted arithmetic mean of the average annual TFPG obtained from best regression (regression 1) for both the variables Y and Z. In Table 4.6 we present the nine industry average for the entire as well as the sub-periods.

From Tables 4.6 we notice that the average annual TFPG shows a rise in the second sub-period in comparison to the first in case of Y variable, for the manufacturing sector as a whole. On the other hand, for variable Z, a fall in average annual TFPG in the second half is reported for the same. It may further be pointed out that figures for Y variable are in general higher than those for Z variable for most of the nine industries and this is reflected in the average annual TFPG for the nine industries taken together (Tables 4.2, 4.3, 4.6).

Table 4.6: Average Annual TFPG for all Industries@

Var	*1970-71 to 1987-88*	*1970-71 to 1980-81*	*1981-82 to 1987-88*
Y	2.38	2.12	2.73
Z	1.89	2.30	1.35

Note : Var = Variable.

@ : Based on Tables 4.2 and 4.3.

Earlier estimates of the production function are a few in number and by and large they cover upto the mid-sixties, only exception being Goldar (1986) and Ahluwalia (1991). All the earlier studies including Goldar's are based on time series data and estimate mainly Cobb-Douglas production function. Production function have been estimated mostly for the large scale manufacturing sector. Ahluwalia's (1991) estimate relate to the organised manufacturing sector. Ours study is also for nine major industries of the organised manufacturing sector of the Indian economy for the period 1970-71 to 1987-88.

Hashim and Dadi (1973) estimated Cobb-Douglas production function over the period 1946 to 1964 and 1953 to 1964 for the large scale census sector of Indian manufacturing. The coefficient of time turned out to be positive and significant in both the periods, being 0.025 and 0.031 respectively. It has been criticised by Ahluwalia (1991) in that the coefficient of time incorporates the joint impact of time and other explanatory variables in the regression equation because of multicollinearity. Mehta (1980) estimated production function for twenty-seven industry groups of the large scale manufacturing sector over the period 1953 to 1965. For industries accounting for almost 80 per cent of the value added in manufacturing, the coefficient of labour was either greater than and statistically significant or not significantly different from zero. No clear result was found on the sign and significance of the coefficient of the time variable.

Goldar's (1986) estimate of the Cobb-Douglas production function for the period 1959 to 1979, in case of large scale manufacturing plus electricity sector shows the coefficient of time to be small, positive, but not significantly different from zero. It registers a TFPG of 0.7 per cent per annum. Ahluwalia's (1991) estimate for the same period is 1.6 per cent per annum. Ahluwalia (1991) has estimated trans-log production function for the manufacturing sector and its use based sub-sectors. It would be interesting to quote Ahluwalia regarding the results obtained from regression exercise of the trans-log production function. "These estimates were found to be statistically significantly different from the alternative estimates using the Cobb-Douglas specification. The production analysis shows that there has been negligible and insignificant growth in total factor productivity in the manufacturing sector over the period from 1959-60 to 1982-83 and there is evidence of a distinct upward shift after 1982-83" (Ahluwalia, 1991, p. 195).

So far as the turnaround hypothesis in industrial productivity, also referred to in Chapter 3, for the Indian manufacturing sector is concerned, we notice (see Table 4.6) that Y variable shows a rise in TFPG in the second period compared to the first for all the nine industries considered by us, taken together. Z variable on the other hand does not speak the same. As pointed out in the previous chapter, Ahluwalia's estimate of TFPG in the period of mid-sixties through the seventies was –0.2/–0.3 per cent per annum for the estimates based on trans-log index. Estimating the trans-log production function, she found negligible and insignificant growth in total factor productivity, for the manufacturing sector as a whole, over the period from 1959-60 to 1982-83. Our findings, really, are different. Estimates based on the trans-log production function shows that during the seventies TFPG was positive and quite significant. Acceleration in TFPG in the eighties, for Y variable, is only moderate. In fact, Z variable shows a fall in TFPG in the eighties compared to the seventies. We should note that our analysis is silent about the trend of TFPG within the periods. So, strictly, we cannot talk of a 'turnaround'. We can only compare the average annual TFPG for the two sub-periods. Here our findings are not unambiguous.

Looking at the individual industries, we notice a sharp increase in TFPG, in the second period compared to the first in case of Y variable for Chemical and chemical products, Transport equipment and parts and Food products. A moderate increase is observed for Electricity. TFPG for Y variable remained more or less the same over the sub-periods for Electrical machinery and parts, Non-electrical machinery and Non-metallic mineral products for the same variable. A sharp fall in TFPG in the second period was noticed for Cotton textiles, while Basic metal and alloy registered a moderate fall for Y variable.

In case of Z variable, while a sharp increase in TFPG for the second sub-period is reported for Transport equipment and parts, Chemical and chemical products show only a small increase. Rest of the industries, in general, show a marked decline in TFPG in the second period, except Food products, where TFPG remained the same over the two sub-periods. Thus important industries (in terms of share in the total manufacturing production) such as Electricity, Basic metal and alloy, Electrical machinery etc showed a sharp decline in TFPG in the second period compared to the first. Considering eighteen cases, two for each industry corresponding to the two variables Y and Z, we notice that, while a sharp fall in TFPG in the second period compared to the first is observed in seven cases, a sharp rise is shown for four cases. Moderate rise or fall in TFPG in the second period is noticed for two and one case respectively. In four cases, TFPG remained more or less the same over the sub-periods.

VI. GROWTH ACCOUNTING

In this section we have tried to give an explanation of the growth of output of various industries in terms of the contributions of the growth in the factor inputs and total factor productivity. Table 4.7 presents TFPG obtained from the first regression and output growth for both the variables Y and Z with respect to nine industries under study. To facilitate comparison the growth of factor inputs, labour and capital are also shown in the said table.

Table 4.7: Growth Rates of Output, Labour, Capital and TFP

Industry		*Output*	*Labour*	*Capital*	*TFP*
1	Y	3.77	1.30	1.76	3:31
	Z	2.40			1.80
2	Y	4.16	1.90	2.51	3.53
	Z	4.06			3.06
3	Y	2.94	1.16	2.57	2.93
	Z	2.06			1.72
4	Y	2.70	0.99	2.96	2.34
	Z	2.56			3.54
5	Y	3.82	1.47	1.03	2.08
	Z	2.66			1.67
6	Y	3.00	1.15	1.38	2.41
	Z	2.59			2.56
7	Y	2.74	1.50	3.46	1.77
	Z	3.33			0.98
8	Y	1.19	--0.05	1.60	0.03
	Z	-0.28			-0.28
9	Y	1.92	0.70	1.42	0.64
	Z	2.35			0.34

Note: Industry numbers as in earlier tables.
Y = Variable Y, Z = Variable Z.

Tables 4.8 and 4.9 shows the contribution of the growth in inputs (capital and labour) and that of total factor productivity to the growth of output of the nine industries concerned, for variables Y and Z respectively. The approach to the computation of the contributions of growth in factor inputs and TFPG towards the growth in output has been discussed in great detail in Chapter 2. Contrary to the results of other studies as mentioned earlier in this chapter, our finding is that TFPG plays an important role in the growth of output of the organised manufacturing sector in India. From Tables 4.8 and 4.9 we notice that the combined contributions of capital and labour to output growth for a few industries (mainly for the Z variable) to be very low and even zero or negative. It may be mentioned here that a negative or zero contribution of a factor does not mean that it was unimportant in the production process. It only means that on the margine the factors were rather unproductive. Thus, a zero contribution of capital stock in period 't' could be, or was in fact, achieved without capital explanation in that period, but that may not imply that the growth in 't' could be achieved without capital expansion in 't-1' even if capital's contribution in 't-1' was also zero.

Table 4.8: Share of TFP and Inputs in Growth (%)

Industry	*Growth in Y*	*TFPG*	*Inputs #*
1.	3.77	3.31	0.46
2.	4.16	3.53	0.63
3.	2.94	2.93	0.01
4.	2.70	2.34	0.36
5.	3.82	2.08	1.74
6.	3.00	2.41	0.59
7.	2.74	1.77	0.97
8.	1.19	0.03	1.16
9.	1.92	0.64	1.28

Note : Industry numbers as in earlier tables.
: Capital and Labour jointly.

From Table 4.8, for variable Y, we observe that while the highest contribution to output growth in terms of TFPG occurs for Basic metal and alloy, Cotton textiles turns up last. TFPG explains more than eighty per cent of output growth for Chemical and chemical products, Electricity, Basic metal and alloy, Transport equipment and parts and Non-electrical machinery. The contribution of TFPG towards output growth is between fifty and sixty-five per cent in case of Electrical machinery and parts and Non-metallic mineral products. It is low and less than thirty-five per cent for Cotton textiles and Food products.

Table 4.9: Share of TFP and Inputs in Growth (%)

Industry	*Growth in Z*	*TFPG*	*Inputs #*
1.	2.40	1.80	0.60
2.	4.06	3.06	1.00
3.	2.06	1.72	0.34
4.	2.56	3.54	0.98
5.	2.66	1.67	0.99
6.	2.59	2.56	0.03
7.	3.33	0.98	2.35
8.	−0.28	−0.28	0.00
9.	2.35	0.34	2.01

Note : Notations as in Table 4.8.

: Capital and Labour Jointly.

In case of variable Z, though output growth for Cotton textiles turns out to be negative, TFPG also is negative by the same magnitude and hence explains the whole of output growth. TFPG explains more than eighty per cent of output growth for Basic metal and alloy, Cotton textiles and Non-electrical machinery. It contributes between sixty to eighty per cent, towards output growth, for Chemical and chemical products, Electricity, Transport equipment and parts and Electrical machinery. It is less than thirty per cent for Non-metallic mineral products and Food products, the latter showing the lowest contribution.

As pointed out earlier, we may consider the aggregate of the nine industries to represent roughly the overall manufacturing sector. Table 4.10 shows the weighted arithmetic means of the output growth, TFPG and the contribution of inputs (capital plus labour) for both the variables Y and Z. We notice from Table 4.10 that the estimates for variable Y is of higher magnitude than that of variable

Z. It is clear from Table 4.10 that in a broad perspective, for the manufacturing sector as a whole, TFPG explains 76.77 and 75.10 per cent of the growth in manufacturing output for Y and Z variables respectively. Corresponding estimates of the joint contribution of capital and labour turned out to be 23.23 and 24.90 per cent. In other words, our estimates suggest that TFPG explains three-fourths of output growth of the part (80%) of the registered manufacturing sector of India over the period 1970-71 to 1987-88. This result is in sharp contrast with others' findings and this result is supported by both of our measures of output.

Table 4.10: Contributions of TFPG and Growth in Inputs to Growth in Manufacturing Output (%)

Variable	*Output*	*TFPG*	*Inputs #*
Y	3.10	2.38	0.72
Z	2.53	1.90	0.63

Note : # : Capital and Labour jointly.

NOTE

1. Strictly speaking this is not proper. The nine industries accounted for a little more than three-fourths of the value added in 1982-83 in the registered manufacturing sector.

Appendix to Chapter 4

Table 4A.1: Estimates of Production Function for Chemical and Chemical Products

Dependent Variable:			*Log Y*			*Log Z*
Explanatory Variables	*Reg.1*	*Reg.2*	*Reg.3*	*Reg.4*	*Reg.5*	*Reg.1*
Log K	–21.94	–21.56			0.81	
	(3.77)	(3.71)			(166)	
Log L						2.08
						(5.14)
Time	0.70	0.69	0.116	0.113	0.154	
	(6.20)	(6.16)	(8.39)	(7.79)	(4.53)	
Log K^2	4.82	4.71	0.235	0.171		0.33
	(4.04)	(3.95)	(11.6)	(9.79)		(8.86)
Log L^2		–0.07		-0.12		
		(12.34)		(9.36)		
$Time^2$	0.0029	0.0029				
	(5.00)	(5.00)				
Log K.time	–028	–0.27	–0.072	–0.07		
	(5.88)	(5.84)	(9.10)	(8.68)		
Log L.time			0.059	0.059	-0.07	0.01
			(4.48)	(4.25)	(3.84)	(3.41)
Log K.Log L	–0.109		–0.173			-0.81
	(12.29)		(9.76)			(4.65)
Dummy.time			–0.005	–0.01		
			(4.16)	(3.91)		
Intercept	27.23	26.76	1.27	1.278		
	(3.83)	(3.78)	(14.1)	(13.6)		
DW	2.19	2.21	2.80	2.80	2.45	1.83
R^2	0.9996	0.9996	0.9996	0.999	0.993	0.945

Note: Dummy = D10 : Takes the value zero upto ninth observation and one from tenth observation onwards. Reg. = Regression. Figures in parentheses are t–values.

Table 4A.2: Estimates of Production Function for Electricity

Dependent Variable: Explanatory Variables	*Log Y*		*Log Z*
	Reg. 1	*Reg. 2*	*Reg. 1*
Log K	1.168	0.6858	
	(7.12)	(106.87)	
Log L			
Time			0.433
			(3.73)
Log K^2			
Log L^2	0.6998		
	(4.51)		
$Time^2$			
Log K.Time			
Log L.Time	0.0173	0.0118	-0.217
	(6.52)	(10.58)	(3.75)
Log K.Log L	-0.6912		0.358
	(4.30)		(41.64)
Dummy.Time			0.0137
			(2.20)
Intercept			
DW	2.03	1.50	2.70
R^2	0.988	0.965	0.9496

Note: Dummy = D9 : Takes the value zero upto eighth observation and one from ninth observation onwards. Reg. = Regression.

Figures in parentheses are t–values.

Table 4A.3: Estimates of Production Function for Basic Metal and Alloy

Dependent Variable: Explanatory *Variables*	*Log Y* *Reg.1*	*Reg.2*	*Log Z* *Reg.1*	*Reg.2*
Log K	0.2375		−1.898	
	(2.27)		(2.80)	
Log L				
Time			0.431	0.531
			(2.94)	(5.18)
Log K²		0.0471		-0.471
		(2.23)		(4.43)
Log L²				
Time²				
Log K.Time	−0.0607	−0.061		
	(3.30)	(3.30)		
Log L.Time	0.1039	0.1043	−0.234	−0.29
	(3.72)	(3.71)	(2.87)	(5.34)
Log K.Log L			0.897	1.148
			(3.30)	(7.59)
Dummy.Time			0.0094	0.013
			(2.04)	(3.22)
Intercept	1.3977	1.697	2.891	
	(5.41)	(3.91)	(4.63)	
DW	1.65	1.63	2.59	2.37
R^2	0.982	0.982	0.937	0.912

Note : Notations as in Table 4A.2.

Table 4A.4: Estimates of Production Function for Transport Equipment and Parts

Dependent Variable: Explanatory *Variables*	*Log Y*		*Log Z*
	Reg.1	*Reg.2*	*Reg.1*
Log K	1.6638		-11.19
	(57.8)		(2.60)
Log L		1.9163	-11.43
		(17.99)	(2.62)
Time			0.9475
			(3.85)
Log K^2	-0.3703		
	(23.3)		
Log L^2		-0.50	
		(7.64)	
$Time^2$			0.0075
			(4.51)
Log K.Time		0.01	-0.272
		(17.23)	(5.59)
Log L.Time	0.0094		-0.28
	(8.2)		(2.39)
Log K.Log L			7.78
			(2.91)
Dummy.Time	0.0126		-0.021
	(5.1)		(2.77)
Intercept	0.1221		17.53
	(4.05)		(2.50)
DW	2.00	1.39	2.97
R^2	0.9943	0.9896	0.991

Note : Notation as in Table 4A.1.

Table 4A.5: Estimates of Production Function for Electrical Machinery and Parts

Dependent Variable: Explanatory *Variables*	*Log Y* *Reg.1*	*Reg.2*	*Log Z* *Reg.1*
Log K			–22.1
			(2.22)
Log L	1.0722		–28.98
	(140.66)		(2.14)
Time			0.404
			((2.08)
Log K^2		–0.3464	
		(7.80)	
Log L^2			
$Time^2$		0.0003	
		(3.73)	
Log K.Time	0.0108		–0.1997
	(19.78)		(2.03)
Log L.Time			
Log K.Log L		1.032	15.22
		(18.64)	(2.22)
Dummy.Time			
Intercept			43.79
			(2.22)
DW	1.946	2.06	3.01
R^2	0.9889	0.984	0.982

Note : Notations as in Table 4A.1.

Table 4A.6: Estimates of Production Function for Non-Electrical Machineries

Dependent Variable: Explanatory *Variables*	*Log Y* *Reg.1*	*Reg.2*	*Log Z* *Reg.1*	*Reg.2*
Log K	0.5180		1.89	1.454
	(4.51)		(7.65)	(6.65)
Log L	1.0403			
	(10.62)			
Time				0.061
				(7.59)
Log K^2				
Log L^2				
$Time^2$			–0.0025	–0.002
			(8.27)	(7.48)
Log K.Time		-0.0237		
		(3.57)		
Log L.Time	0.014	0.044	0.043	
	(11.1)	(5.46)	(8.29)	
Log K.Log L	–0.307	0.12	–0.652	–0.371
	(3.51)	(2.67)	(4.04)	(2.60)
Dummy.Time				
Intercept		1.34		
		(10.08)		
DW	2.47	2.69	2.52	2.37
R^2	0.994	0.995	0.985	0.983

Note : Notations as in Table 4A.2.

Table 4A.7: Estimates of Production Function for Non-Metallic Mineral Products

Dependent Variable:	*Log Y*					*Log Z*
Explanatory Variables	*Reg.1*	*Reg.2*	*Reg.3*	*Reg.4*	*Reg.5*	*Reg.1*
Log K	0.89	0.77	0.79	0.29		4.32
	(5.57)	(5.12)	(5.34)	(7.91)		(3.14)
Log L	0.52	0.54	0.495			
	(13.2)	(14.5)	(11.9)			
Time		0.02	0.021			–0.61
Log K^2		(5.78)	(5.09)			(2.78)
Log L^2						
$Time^2$						–.006
						(4.76)
Log K.Time						
Log L.Time	0.014			0.012	0.008	0.46
	(6.01)			(11.1)	(5.84)	(2.99)
Log K.Log L	–0.356	–0.28	–0.27		0.154	–2.37
	(3.51)	(3.06)	(2.99)		(6.05)	(2.57)
Dummy.Time	–0.004	–0.03	–0.003	–0.004		
	(2.56)	(2.26)	(2.37)	(2.23)		
Intercept				0.917	1.035	
				(14.5)	(16.7)	
DW	2.30	2.19	2.31	2.31	1.64	1.61
R^2	0.994	0.993	0.993	0.993	0.988	0.974

Note : Notations as in Table 4A.2.

Table 4A.8: Estimates of Production Function for Cotton Textiles

Dependent Variable: Explanatory *Variables*	*Log Y*		*Log Z*
	Reg.1	*Reg.2*	*Reg.1*
Log K			
Log L	–54.42 (4.58)	0.999 (151.1)	–140.5 (6.12)
Time			–0.986 (7.39)
Log K^2			
Log L^2	13.44 (4.66)		34.04 (6.12)
$Time^2$	–0.002 (3.55)		
Log K.Time	–0.0634 (4.43)	0.0321 (4.03)	0.148 (4.81)
Log L.Time	–0.047 (3.50)	–0.028 (3.1)	0.332 (5.80)
Log K.Log L			
Dummy.Time			–0.165 (4.95)
Intercept	57.07 (4.67)		147.05 (6.20)
DW	2.26	1.89	2.58
R^2	0.978	0.924	0.92

Note : Notations as in Table 4A.1.

Table 4A.9: Estimates of Production Function for Food Products

Dependent Variable	*Log Y*	*Log Z*
Explanatory Variables	*Reg.1*	*Reg.1*
Log K	–32.95	
	(3.88)	
Log L	28.9	0.938
	(3.89)	(58.5)
Time	1.23	
	(3.69)	
Log K^2	9.41	
	(4.04)	
Log L^2	–6.90	
	(3.85)	
$Time^2$	0.007	
	(3.94)	
Log K.Time	–0.643	0.087
	(3.78)	(7.31)
Log L.Time		–0.086
		(6.63)
Log K.Log L		
Dummy.Time		
Intercept		
DW	2.28	1.08
R^2	0.928	0.879

Note : Notations as in Table 4A.1.

Output Growth and TFPG
Variable : Y

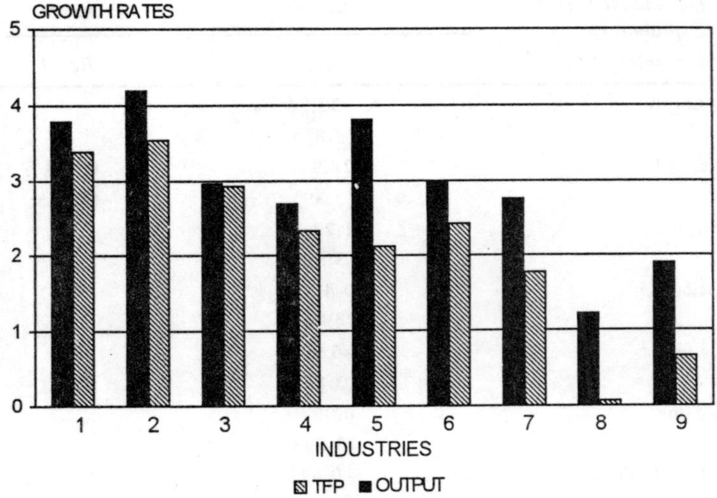

Output Growth and TFPG
Variable : Z

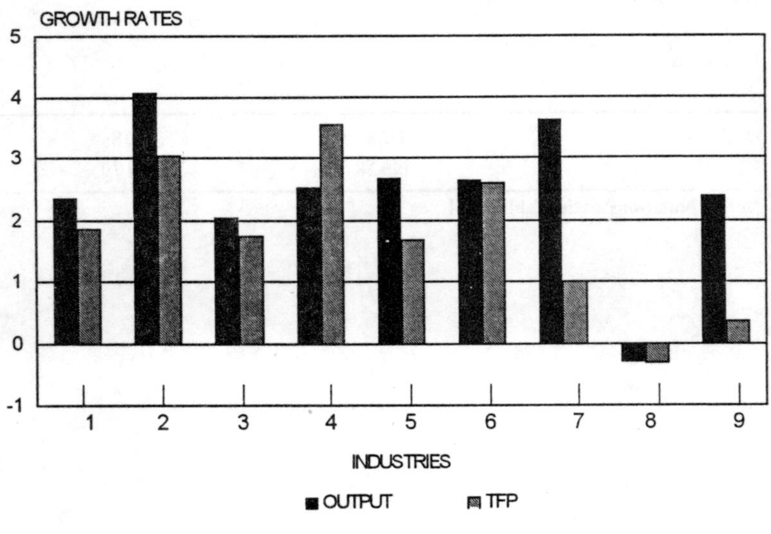

Average Annual TFPG
Production Function Approach

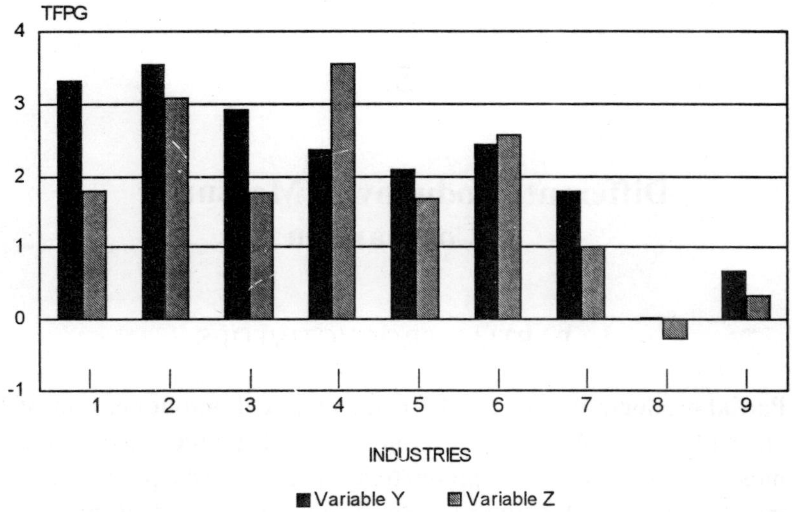

5

Different Productivity Measures: A Comparison

I. PARTIAL PRODUCTIVITIES

Partial productivity indices defined as the real output per unit of any particular real input like labour or capital, are the simplest and most intuitive measures of productivity. Thus, we have productivity measures such as, labour productivity and capital productivity.

One point to be noted in the context of partial productivity analysis, is that it tends to depend, to a great extent, on capital intensity. Increase in labour productivity may be due to improved efficiency or technological progress or more capital per unit of labour. Of course, these possible events are not mutually exclusive. Specifically, labour productivity may increase because of factors such as learning by doing, improved skills, etc., or because there are probably better and/or more machines to work with. Thus, it may be thought that in a situation where capital intensity is increasing over time, the analysis of partial productivity changes would overstate the increase in labour productivity in the sense that the same quality of labour hour with basically no change in technological knowledge will now be found to be more productive. Clearly, the concept of partial labour productivity is simply how much an average labour unit is producing and we go from here to ask how this productivity changes over time. The question whether an increase in partial labour productivity has been possible because of technical progress or capital deepening (rise in capital-labour ratio) is not most relevant here. The question is, no doubt, important and can be better tackled by other methods of productivity analysis (see Chapters 3 and 4). Similarly, partial capital productivity seeks to project how much an average unit of capital produces.

We may note one point here. If there is no technical progress and there is constant returns to scale, capital deepening will lead to rise in partial labour productivity and fall in partial capital productivity. This is the lesson from neo-classical production function assuming constant level of capacity utilisation. So one tends to conclude that there is increasing return to scale and/or technical progress when both capital and labour productivity increases.

We have two sets of labour and capital productivity indices corresponding to two different measures of real value added represented by Y and Z. We have also looked into the changes in capital intensity (capital-labour ratio). Tables 5A.1 to 5A.9 show the partial productivity indices for two variables Y and Z as well as capital-labour ratio, for all the nine industries that have been taken up for this study.

We have estimated semi-logarithmic time trend for the partial productivities as well as capital-labour ratio. Table 5.1 shows the regression results. From Table 5.1 we observe a positive and significant trend for capital productivity in case of variable Y, for Chemical and chemical products, Electricity, Electrical machinery and parts and Non-electrical machineries. No statistically significant trend is observed for rest of the industries. Significant positive trend in case of variable Z is noticed for Chemical and chemical products, Electricity, Electrical machinery, Non-electrical machinery and Food products. Negative and significant trend is observed for Cotton textiles. Rest of the industries do not show any significant trend.

So far as labour productivity is concerned, we notice positive and significant trend in case of variable Y, for all the industries. Similar observation is true for all the industries except Cotton textiles in case of variable Z. Thus, for a number of industries, both for variables Y and Z, both capital and labour productivities show positive and significant trend.

Table 5.1: Regression Estimates for Trend in Capital and Labour Productivity and Capital Intensity

Indry.	*Variable : Y*		*Variable : Z*		*Cap-Lab Ratio*
	Cap. prod.	*Lab. prod*	*Cap. prod*	*Lab. prod*	
1.	0.0195 (16.25)	0.0197 (19.7)	0.0064 (3.05)	0.0066 (3.88)	0.0002 (0.13)
2.	0.0164 (5.86)	0.0226 (14.13)	0.0151 (3.68)	0.0213 (5.76)	0.0062 (2.95)
3.	0.0037 (1.32)	0.0177 (14.83)	−0.0051 (−1.50)	0.0089 (4.05)	0.0140 (5.83)
4.	−0.0024 (−0.63)	0.0172 (10.75)	−0.0038 (−1.12)	0.0157 (12.08)	0.0195 (5.28)
5.	0.0275 (8.87)	0.234 (21.27)	0.0161 (4.88)	0.0120 (10.00)	−0.0041 (−1.17)
6.	0.0370 (9.49)	0.0083 (16.6)	0.0140 (·6.41)	0.0145 (11.15)	0.0004 (0.18)
7.	−0.0070 (−1.80)	0.0123 (6.15)	−0.0014 (−0.31)	0.0180 (7.5)	0.0194 (3.46)
8.	−0.0041 (−1.71)	0.0176 (12.57)	−0.0191 (−5.62)	0.0026 (0.93)	0.0217 (8.04)
9.	0.0047 (1.62)	0.0121 (2.12)	0.0089 (4.24)	0.0164 (2.93)	0.0074 (1.42)

Note: Results obtained from semi-logarithmic trend analysis. Figures in brackets refer to trend t-statistics for the trend coefficients. Cap. prod = Capital productivity, Lab. prod = Labour productivity, Cap-Lab Ratio = Capital-labour ratio.

Industry 1: Chemical & Chemical Products. 2: Electricity. 3: Basic Metal & Alloys. 4: Transport Equipment & Parts. 5: Electrical Machinery & Parts. 6: Non-Electrical Machinery. 7: Non-Metallic Mineral Products. 8: Cotton Textiles. 9: Food Products. Indry. = Industry.

As indicated above, trend in capital-labour ratio plays a significant role in the analysis of partial productivity estimates. It is observed from Table 5.1, that a positive and significant trend in capital-labour ratio (capital intensity) for Electricity, Basic metal and alloy, Transport equipment and parts, Non-metallic mineral products and Cotton textiles. Significant trend is not seen for rest of the industries.

Table 5.2: Trend in Partial Productivities and Capital Intensity

	Variable : Y		*Variable : Z*		*Capital*
Indry.	*Cap. prod*	*Lab. prod*	*Cap. prod*	*Lab.prod*	*Intensity*
1.	+ve	+ve	+ve	+ve	No trend
2.	+ve	+ve	+ve	+ve	+ve
3.	No trend	+ve	No trend	+ve	+ve
4.	No trend	+ve	No trend	+ve	+ve
5.	+ve	+ve	+ve	+ve	No trend
6.	+ve	+ve	+ve	+ve	No trend
7.	No trend	+ve	No trend	+ve	+ve
8.	No trend	+ve	-ve	No trend	+ve
9.	No trend	+ve	+ve	+ve	No trend

Note: Industry 1: Chemical & Chemical Products. 2: Electricity. 3: Basic Metal & Alloys. 4: Transport Equipment & Parts. 5: Electrical Machinery & Parts. 6: Non-Electrical Machinery. 7: Non-Metallic Mineral Products. 8: Cotton Textiles. 9: Food Products. Indry. = Industry.
Cap. prod: Capital Productivity.
Lab. prod: Labour Productivity

Clearly, for a number of industries capital intensity has increased over time. As expected, we observe a concurrent increase in partial labour productivity. What is more, we have also observed a simultaneous increase in capital productivity in a number of industries. This leads to the strong inference that technical progress had a significant presence in these industries. Of course, this is not to suggest that technical progress was insignificant in other industries where all the above trends were not simultaneously present. We want to note here that for Cotton textiles in the case of Z-measure of output, the finding that partial capital productivity was declining with partial labour productivity showing no trend in spite of a positive trend in capital intensity corroborates our findings in Chapters 3 and 4 that TFPG for the case was negative by all approaches.

II. COMPARISON AMONG ESTIMATES

In this section, we have tried to focus on the similarities and dissimilarities in the estimates of total factor productivity growth (TFPG) arrived at from different approaches discussed in the previous chapters. Though, the approaches to the various estimates of TFPG have been discussed in great detail in Chapter 2, it would be worthwhile here, to present a brief analysis of the dissimilarities among the alternative approaches.

In the case of the conventional estimates of TFPG (Kendrick, Solow and Trans-log) the approach is to equate the factor prices with the respective marginal productivities so that the factor shares in output are the respective elasticities. More generally, they require an environment of competitive equilibrium in the sense that, the economy allocates the resources efficiently, so that each factor is paid just the marginal product and there exists constant returns to scale, so that payment according to marginal productivity exhausts the product. The production function approach to the estimation of TFPG does not require the above mentioned restrictive assumptions to prevail in the economy. Various researchers have estimated different forms of production function. We have started with the general trans-log production function and arrived at our best-fit production function through a process of backward elimination and three-fold test as discussed in Chapter 2.

Keeping in mind the above differences between various estimates of TFPG we may now proceed to have a detailed comparison between the conventional estimates and estimates through production function. Comparison between the above approaches may be on the following counts: (i) average annual TFPG, (ii) changes in the estimates over the sub-periods, (iii) estimates for the overall manufacturing sector for the entire period of our study, (iv) proportional contribution to output growth, (v) rank correlation.

So far as the average annual TFPG is concerned, we notice disparities among the estimates obtained from different approaches. Tables 3.1 and 4.2 show that the estimates of average annual TFPG from best regression (marked Reg. 1 in Table 4.2) for variable Y are in general greater than those obtained from Kendrick index of TFPG. Exceptions, though few, occur in the case of Electrical machinery and parts and Cotton textiles. The estimates from Solow and Trans-log measures of TFPG are very close to those for Kendrick measure. Comparing the estimates of second regression with that of Kendrick, Solow and Trans-log indices the above observation remains more or less valid, but the exceptions arises in case of Electricity apart from the cases of Electrical machinery and Cotton textiles. Point to be stressed here is that whereas the gap between the estimates widens to a large extent for Electrical machinery and Electricity, it diminishes significantly in case of Cotton textiles. The observation that TFPG estimates from regression analysis are higher than those obtained from conventional approaches (Kendrick, Solow and Trans-log) also applies for the other three regressions (regressions 3, 4 and 5, Tables 3.1 and 4.2) for Chemical and chemical products and Non-metallic mineral products.

General observation for variable Z is in line with that for variable Y. Exceptions in case of variable Z occur for Cotton textiles and Food products. Significant point to be noted here is that estimates for Y variable in case of both the production function and other conventional approaches are in general higher than their counterparts for variable Z. Exceptions in case of Kendrick, Solow and Trans-log indices occur for Non-metallic mineral products and Food products. In case of regression analysis, Transport equipment and parts and Non-electrical machinery come out as the exceptions. It may be noted that the above findings remain true for the second regression obtained for Basic metal and alloy and Non-electrical machinery for variable Z.

III. CHANGE IN TFPG OVER SUB-PERIODS

A detailed discussion on the estimates of TFPG over the sub-periods has been made in Chapters 3 and 4. Here we present a comparison between estimates obtained through Kendrick, Solow and Trans-log approaches on the one hand and the production function approach on the other hand. As noted in Chapter 3, though Kendrick measure shows a resemblance with those by Solow and Trans-log approaches for the entire period of our study, the picture is not the same with regard to changes in TFPG between the sub-periods[1]. So far as the estimates of Kendrick, Solow and Trans-log indices of TFPG are concerned, we observe that in more than fifty-five per cent cases TFPG declines in the second period compared to the first, considering both the variables Y and Z. In our regression approach the figure for the best regression is fifty per cent.

If we consider the aggregate of nine industries to represent roughly the overall manufacturing sector, we have a scope of comparison between different approaches to the estimation of TFPG. Table 5.3 presents the arithmetic mean of annual TFPG according to all the approaches for both Y and Z variables. We present the nine-industry average for the whole period as well as the sub-periods.

Table 5.3 shows that the estimates of TFPG for the overall manufacturing sector obtained from regression analysis are higher in magnitude than those of Kendrick, Solow and Trans-log indices. Point to be noted here is that, excepting for the estimate of sub-period B for Z variable, figures for variable Y are greater than their counterparts in case of variable Z.

Table 5.3: Average Annual TFPG for all the Industries (in percentages)

	Variable : Y			*Variable : Z*		
Different Measures	*A*	*B*	*C*	*A*	*B*	*C*
Kendrick	1.60	1.45	1.83	1.02	1.17	1.01
Solow	1.57	1.44	1.89	0.91	0.92	0.86
Trans-log	1.56	1.38	1.93	0.89	0.85	0.90
Prod. Fn.	2.38	2.12	2.73	1.89	2.30	1.35

Note: A: 1970-71 to 1987-88. B: 1970-71 to 1980-81. C: 1981-82 to 1987-88. Prod. Fn. = Production function.

As regards comparison of our estimates with those of other studies, we notice wide variation. As is noted in Table 3.3, our estimates of Kendrick, Solow and Trans-log measures of TFPG, for variable Y, during the seventies show close resemblance to their counterpart presented by Goldar (1986). However the above observation does not apply for the variable Z. Marked differences in the estimates is also registered when Goldar's study is compared with our results obtained by regression exercises. Similarly, as regards estimates obtained through regression analysis, our results vary from those obtained by Goldar (1986) and Ahluwalia (1991).

With regard to changes in average annual TFPG over the sub-periods the estimates of Kendrick, Solow and Trans-log measures of TFPG for variable Y show a rise in TFPG in the second sub-period compared to the first. The same is true of the estimates through the production function approach. However, variable Z does not project a uniform picture for the different estimates. We would like to note here, as mentioned in Chapter 2, that we are inclined to treat the Y-measure of output as more reliable than the Z-measure.

IV. GROWTH ACCOUNTING AND RANK CORRELATIONS

It would now be interesting to observe the differences in the estimates of the contributions of TFPG and joint growth of factor inputs, capital and labour, towards the growth in output computed from different approaches. Table 5.4 presents the same for the overall manufacturing sector.

A glance at Table 5.4 shows that TFPG explains 76.77 and 75.10 per cent of the growth in manufacturing output in case of regression analysis for the variables Y and Z respectively. Corresponding figures in case of Kendrick index are 51.61 and 40.32 for variables Y and Z respectively, 50.65 and 40 for Y and Z variables for Solow index and 50.32 and 35.57 for Y and Z for Trans-log index.

Table 5.4: Contributions of TFPG and Growth in Inputs in Manufacturing Output (%)

Different Measures	*Variable : Y*			*Variable : Z*		
	O.G	*TFPG*	*(K+L)*	*O.G.*	*TFPG*	*(K+L)*
Kendrick	3.10	1.60	1.50	2.53	1.02	1.51
Solow	3.10	1.57	1.53	2.53	0.91	1.62
Trans-log	3.10	1.56	1.54	2.53	0.90	1.63
Prod. Fn.	3.10	2.38	0.72	2.53	1.90	0.63

Note: O.G. : Output growth. (K+L) : Joint Contribution of Capital and Labour. Prod. Fn. = Production function.

Thus, for the manufacturing sector as a whole, regression analysis comes out with significantly high contribution from TFPG towards growth of manufacturing output. Other estimates of TFPG for Y variable show almost equal contributions towards output growth from TFPG and inputs. However, TFPG explains less than fifty per cent of the growth in output in case of variables Z, for the Kendrick, Solow and Trans-log estimates. Production function approach, of course, projects the same picture for Z variable as for Y variable so far proportional contribution of TFPG and inputs to growth of output is concerned.

Table 5.5: Ranking of Industries according to TFPG

	Variable : Y				*Variable : Z*			
IND	*P.FN*	*KEN*	*SOLO*	*TLOG*	*P.FN*	*KEN*	*SOLO*	*TLOG*
ELE	1	2	2	2	2	1	1	1
CCP	2	4	3.5	4	4	6	6	6
BMA	3	6	7	7	5	7	7	7
NEM	4	3	3.5	3	3	2	2	2.5
TEP	5	5	5	6	1	4	4	4
EMP	6	1	1	1	6	3	3	2.5
NMMP	7	9	8	8	7	8	8	8
FP	8	8	9	9	8	5	5	5
CT	9	7	6	5	9	9	9	9

Notes : IND: Industry, ELE: Electricity. CCP: Chemical and Chemical Products. BMA: Basic Metal and Alloy. NEM: Non-Electrical Machinery. TEP: Transport Equipment and Parts. EMP: Electrical Machinery and Parts. NMMP: Non-Metallic Mineral Products. FP. Food Products. CT: Cotton Textiles.

P.FN: Production function measure. KEN: Kendrick Measure. SOLO: Solow measure. TLOG: Trans-log measure.

Table 5.5 presents the ranking of various industries with respect to average annual TFPG for various approaches. As presented in Chapter 4, looking at Table 5.5 we see that the group of top five industries ranked according to TFPG obtained from regression analysis for variables Y and Z are identical. Again, industries with ranks from 6 to 9 according to TFPG obtained from regression analysis for both Y and Z estimates of output are identical. Very close results (though not identical), as regards ranking from all the measures of TFPG, are observed only for two industries: (i) Electricity, which has a rank either one or two, and (ii) Non-metallic mineral products, which has a rank either 7 or 8 or 9. For Cotton textile ranking are identical (the lowest, 9) for all the measures so far as Z measure of output is concerned. Regression 1 for Y measure of output also gives Cotton textiles the rank 9. But other measures of TFPG for Y variable give Cotton textile ranks 5, 6 and 7. Similarly, for Food products, all measures of TFPG for Y variable give ranks 8 or 9. Regression 1 for Z variable also gives the rank 8. But other measures for the Z variables give rank 5. For other industries the disparity in ranking by different measures is greater.

The rank correlation coefficient between Kendrick and regression estimates for variable Y turns out to be 0.60. Corresponding figure for variable Z is 0.6833. Again, the rank correlation coefficient between Trans-log and regression estimates for variable Y is 0.45. Since, Solow index and Trans-log index show almost identical rankings, the rank correlation coefficient between ranking as per Solow index and regression 1 TFPG estimates is also very close to 0.45. Similarly, in case of variable Z, Solow and Trans-log rankings have close resemblance with that of Kendrick. Hence, the rank correlation coefficient between rankings as per regression 1 and Solow or Trans-log index is also very close to 0.6833.

NOTE

1. In case of our regression analysis, we normally obtain more or less similar changes in TFPG over the sub-periods between the best and second best regression. This shows that the results obtained through regression exercises are more or less stable.

Appendix to Chapter 5

Table 5A.1: Partial Productivity and Capital Intensity Indices
Chemical and Chemical Products

Year	Y/K	Y/L	Z/K	Z/L	K/L
1973-74	1.000	1.000	1.000	1.000	1.000
1974-75	1.080	0.994	1.242	1.143	0.920
1975-76	1.037	0.987	1.148	1.093	0.952
1976-77	1.178	1.077	1.203	1.100	0.914
1977-78	1.198	1.101	1.127	1.036	0.919
1978-79	1.293	1.216	1.322	1.244	0.941
1979-80	1.270	1.157	1.100	1.002	0.911
1981-82	1.417	1.301	1.210	1.111	0.918
1982-83	1.682	1.364	1.424	1.155	0.811
1983-84	1.562	1.446	1.411	1.306	0.926
1984-85	1.750	1.542	1.392	1.226	0.881
1985-86	1.705	1.607	1.305	1.230	0.943
1986-87	1.746	1.787	1.219	1.248	1.024
1987-88	1.811	1.807	1.347	1.343	0.997

Table 5A.2: Partial Productivity and Capital Intensity Indices
Electricity

Year	Y/K	Y/L	Z/K	Z/L	K/L
1973-74	1.000	1.000	1.000	1.000	1.000
1974-75	1.191	1.083	1.063	0.967	0.909
1975-76	1.501	1.204	1.611	1.292	0.802
1976-77	1.424	1.284	1.469	1.325	0.902
1977-78	1.168	1.231	1.320	1.391	1.054
1978-79	1.183	1.317	1.607	1.789	1.114
1979-80	1.233	1.265	1.453	1.492	1.026
1980-81	1.448	1.371	1.434	1.359	0.947
1981-82	1.652	1.606	1.982	1.928	0.973
1982-83	1.604	1.631	1.800	1.830	1.017
1983-84	1.844	1.839	2.242	2.236	0.997
1984-85	1.627	1.611	1.559	1.543	0.990
1985-86	1.708	1.867	1.670	1.826	1.094
1986-87	1.946	2.174	1.995	2.229	1.117
1987-88	1.820	2.169	1.636	1.951	1.192

Table 5A.3: Partial Productivity and Capital Intensity Indices
Basic Metal and Alloys

Year	*Y/K*	*Y/L*	*Z/K*	*Z/L*	*K/L*
1973-74	1.000	1.000	1.000	1.000	1.000
1974-75	1.395	1.126	1.539	1.242	0.807
1975-76	0.981	1.115	1.075	1.221	1.136
1976-77	0.951	1.209	0.039	1.322	1.272
1977-78	0.953	1.238	1.854	1.108	1.298
1978-79	1.114	1.318	1.089	1.288	1.183
1979-80	1.074	1.332	0.978	1.213	1.240
1980-81	1.118	1.394	1.020	1.272	1.247
1981-82	1.201	1.540	1.150	1.474	1.282
1982-83	1.253	1.689	1.038	1.400	1.348
1983-84	1.080	1.487	1.023	1.408	1.376
1984-85	1.080	1.534	0.883	1.254	1.421
1985-86	1.116	1.688	1.085	1.641	1.513
1986-87	1.256	1.791	0.951	1.355	1.426
1987-88	1.179	1.885	0.943	1.509	1.599

Table 5A.4: Partial Productivity and Capital Intensity Indices
Transport Equipment and Parts

Year	*Y/K*	*Y/L*	*Z/K*	*Z/L*	*K/L*
1970-71	0.824	0.855	0.917	0.951	1.038
1971-72	0.911	0.902	1.076	1.066	0.991
1973-74	1.000	1.000	1.000	1.000	1.000
1974-75	1.105	0.944	1.241	1.061	0.855
1975-76	1.115	1.006	1.334	1.204	0.902
1976-77	1.087	1.201	1.223	1.351	1.105
1977-78	1.043	1.160	1.150	1.279	1.112
1978-79	0.567	1.223	0.709	1.529	2.156
1979-80	0.648	1.064	0.792	1.301	1.642
1980-81	0.739	1.123	0.884	1.344	1.520
1981-82	0.845	1.204	1.046	1.491	1.426
1982-83	0.894	1.287	1.115	1.604	1.439
1983-84	0.909	1.338	1.084	1.595	1.472
1984-85	0.860	1.416	0.971	1.598	1.647
1985-86	0.872	1.557	0.910	1.625	1.786
1986-87	0.936	1.720	0.984	1.808	1.838
1987-88	0.935	1.861	0.871	1.735	1.991

Table 5A.5: Partial Productivity and Capital Intensity Indices
Electrical Machinery and Parts

Year	*Y/K*	*Y/L*	*Z/K*	*Z/L*	*K/L*
1970-71	0.540	0.847	0.608	0.953	1.568
1971-72	0.631	0.900	0.702	1.002	1.427
1973-74	1.000	1.000	1.000	1.000	1.000
1974-75	0.868	0.903	0.993	1.033	1.040
1975-76	1.039	0.984	1.255	1.187	0.946
1976-77	1.171	1.146	1.173	1.148	0.978
1977-78	1.188	1.198	1.146	1.156	1.009
1978-79	1.296	1.225	1.255	1.187	0.946
1979-80	1.413	1.222	1.314	1.137	0.865
1980-81	1.611	1.401	1.379	1.199	0.870
1981-82	1.703	1.441	1.396	1.181	0.846
1982-83	1.750	1.639	1.468	1.375	0.937
1983-84	1.545	1.567	1.363	1.382	1.014
1984-85	1.602	1.675	1.532	1.602	1.046
1985-86	1.693	1.774	1.267	1.327	1.048
1986-87	1.745	1.952	1.282	1.435	1.119
1987-88	1.716	2.170	1.256	1.589	1.265

Table 5A.6: Partial Productivity and Capital Intensity Indices
Non-Electrical Machinery

Year	*Y/K*	*Y/L*	*Z/K*	*Z/L*	*K/L*
1969-70	0.741	0.900	0.772	0.938	1.215
1970-71	0.860	0.943	0.895	0.982	1.097
1971-72	0.859	0.963	0.910	1.020	1.122
1973-74	1.000	1.000	1.000	1.000	1.000
1974-75	1.165	1.111	1.204	1.149	0.954
1975-76	1.114	1.089	1.284	1.256	0.978
1976-77	1.233	1.264	1.369	1.403	1.025
1977-78	1.194	1.214	1.237	1.258	1.017
1978-79	1.357	1.300	1.409	1.349	0.958
1979-80	1.389	1.217	1.381	1.210	0.876
1980-81	1.573	1.396	1.531	1.359	0.888
1981-82	1.562	1.379	1.537	1.357	0.883
1982-83	1.591	1.470	1.552	1.435	0.924
1983-84	1.384	1.515	1.385	1.516	1.095
1984-85	1.545	1.670	1.623	1.755	1.081
1985-86	1.328	1.733	1.344	1.754	1.305
1986-87	1.604	1.835	1.455	1.665	1.144
1987-88	1.731	1.939	1.438	1.611	1.120

Table 5A.7: Partial Productivity and Capital Intensity Indices
Non-Metallic Mineral Products

Year	*Y/K*	*Y/L*	*Z/K*	*Z/L*	*K/L*
1970-71	0.845	0.998	1.011	1.194	1.182
1971-72	0.875	1.016	1.055	1.225	1.161
1973-74	1.000	1.000	1.000	1.000	1.000
1974-75	1.115	0.935	1.238	1.038	0.838
1975-76	1.165	0.971	1.494	1.245	0.833
1976-77	1.215	1.079	1.446	1.284	0.888
1977-78	1.319	1.145	1.629	1.414	0.868
1978-79	1.240	0.972	1.597	1.251	0.783
1979-80	1.258	1.005	1.583	1.265	0.799
1980-81	1.149	1.089	1.427	1.353	0.948
1981-82	1.091	1.120	1.336	1.371	1.026
1982-83	1.061	1.160	1.567	1.713	1.094
1983-84	0.830	1.146	1.294	1.787	1.381
1984-85	0.918	1.339	1.430	2.086	1.459
1985-86	0.802	1.480	1.166	2.152	1.846
1986-87	0.720	1.582	0.875	1.922	2.197
1987-88	0.696	1.654	0.862	2.048	2.376

Table 5A.8: Partial Productivity and Capital Intensity Indices
Cotton Textiles

Year	*Y/K*	*Y/L*	*Z/K*	*Z/L*	*K/L*
1973-74	1.000	1.000	1.000	1.000	1.000
1974-75	1.211	1.018	1.062	0.893	0.841
1975-76	1.338	1.091	0.931	0.759	0.815
1976-77	1.307	1.152	0.885	0.780	0.881
1977-78	1.254	1.201	0.902	0.863	0.958
1978-79	1.337	1.275	1.097	1.046	0.954
1979-80	1.301	1.190	1.119	1.023	0.914
1980-81	1.214	1.259	0.959	0.994	1.037
1981-82	1.203	1.269	0.827	0.873	1.055
1982-83	1.106	1.294	0.659	0.771	1.170
1983-84	1.056	1.436	0.705	0.958	1.359
1984-85	1.045	1.572	0.594	0.894	1.504
1985-86	1.074	1.740	0.593	0.961	1.620
1986-87	1.053	1.640	0.642	1.000	1.557
1987-88	1.187	1.846	0.618	0.961	1.555

Table 5A.9: Partial Productivity and Capital Intensity Indices
Food Products

Year	*Y/K*	*Y/L*	*Z/K*	*Z/L*	*K/L*
1970-71	1.308	1.416	1.109	1.200	1.083
1973-74	1.000	1.000	1.000	1.000	1.000
1974-75	1.264	0.861	1.232	0.839	0.681
1975-76	1.421	0.865	1.322	0.804	0.609
1976-77	1.314	0.833	1.311	0.831	0.634
1977-78	1.334	0.956	1.235	0.885	0.717
1978-79	1.660	1.293	1.167	0.909	0.779
1979-80	1.335	0.983	1.171	0.863	0.737
1980-81	1.028	0.669	1.068	0.695	0.651
1981-82	1.332	0.817	1.302	0.798	0.613
1982-83	1.638	1.129	1.472	1.014	0.689
1983-84	1.330	1.361	1.553	1.588	1.023
1984-85	1.356	1.368	1.467	1.480	1.009
1985-86	1.463	1.526	1.516	1.580	1.042
1986-87	1.411	1.611	1.465	1.672	1.142
1987-88	1.499	1.690	1.475	1.662	1.127

Partial Productivity Indices
Chemical and Chemical Products

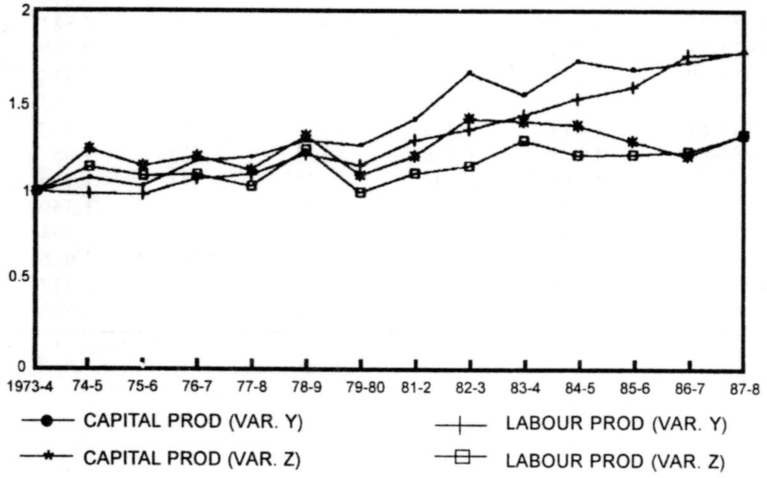

Partial Productivity Indices
Electricity

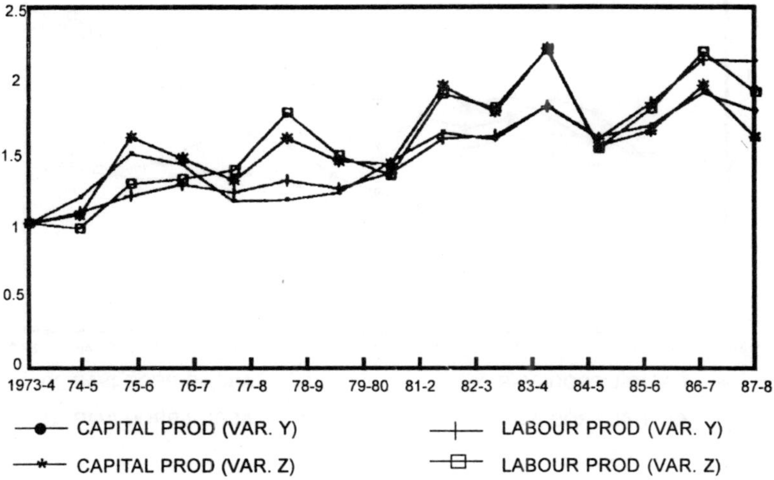

Partial Productivity Indices
Basic Metal and Alloys

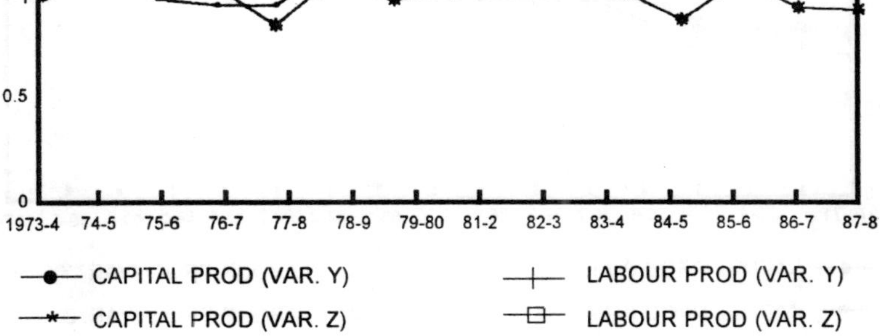

Partial Productivity Indices
Transport Equipment and Parts

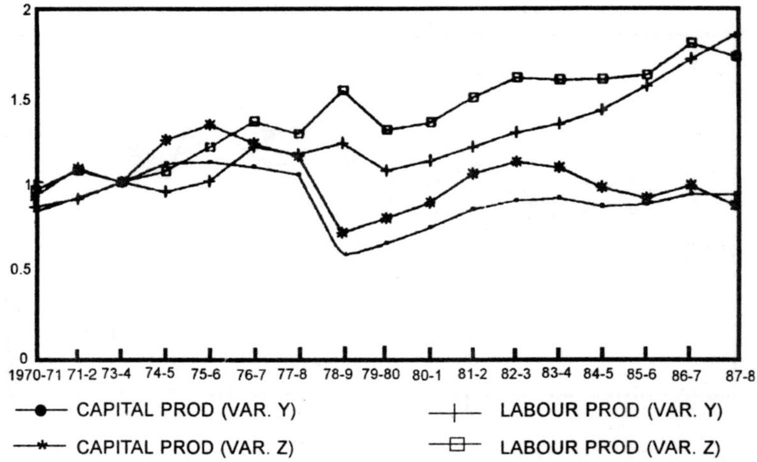

Partial Productivity Indices
Electrical Machinery and Parts

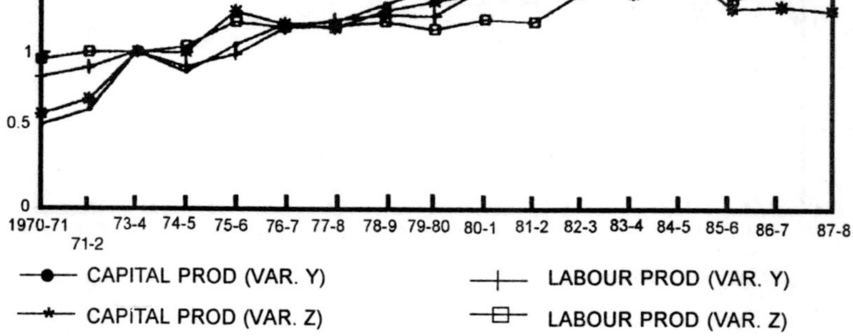

**Partial Productivity Indices
Non-Electrical Machinery**

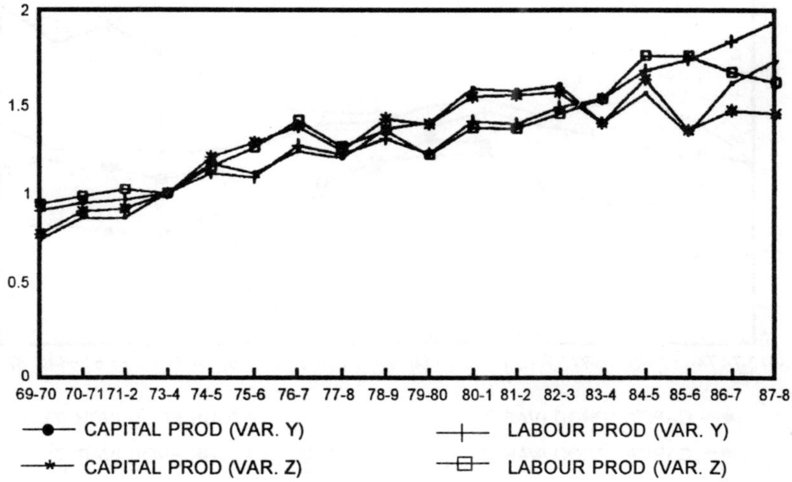

**Partial Productivity Indices
Non-Metallic Mineral Products**

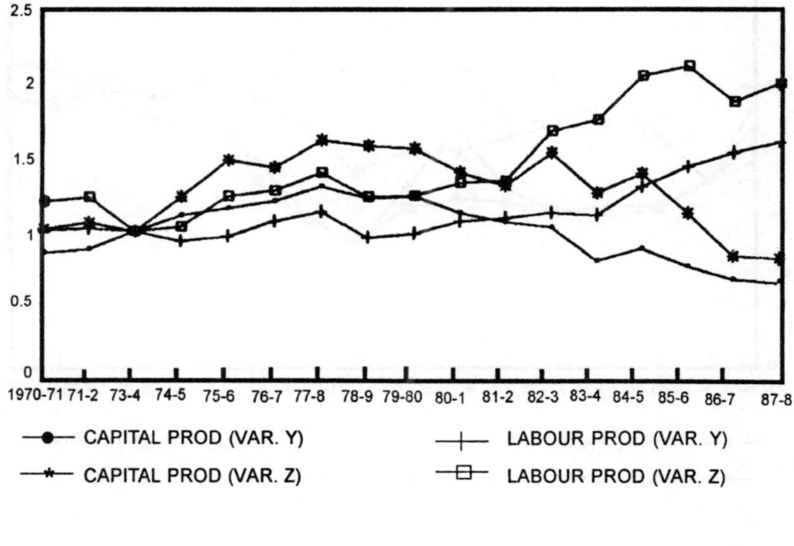

Partial Productivity Indices
Cotton Textiles

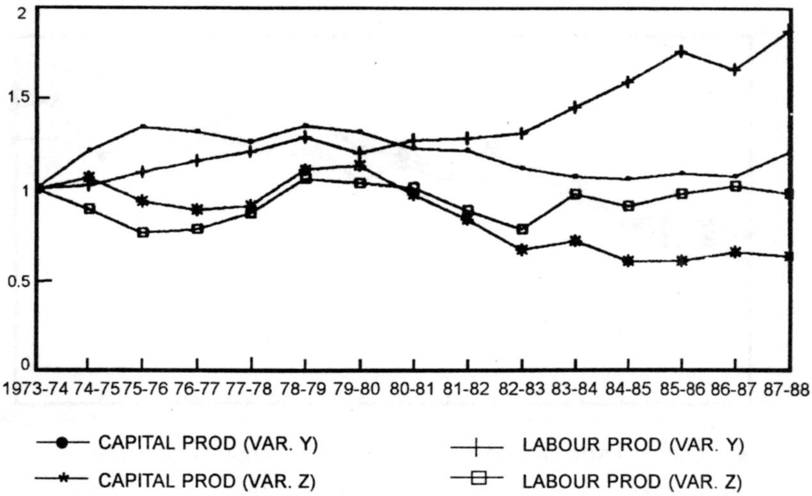

Partial Productivity Indices
Food Products

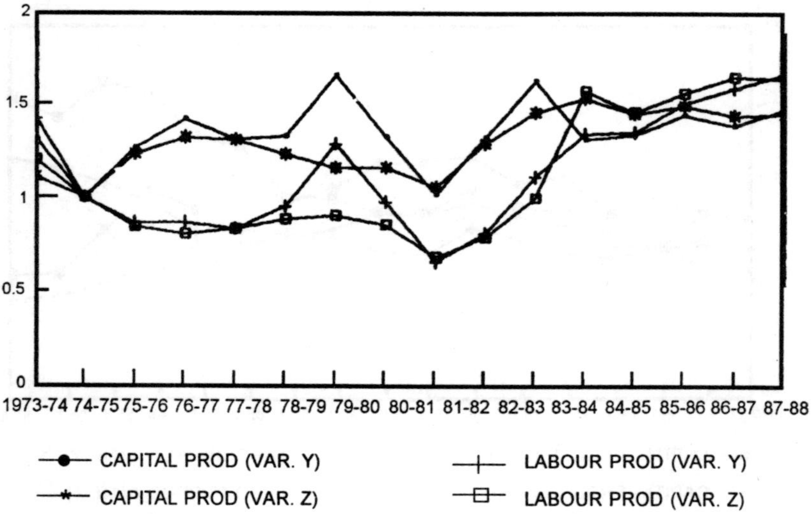

**Average Annual TFPG (Var. Y)
All Industries**

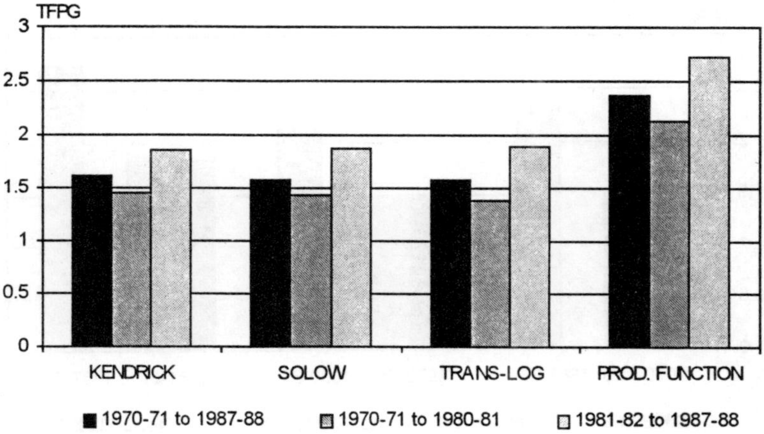

**Average Annual TFPG (Var. Z)
All Industries**

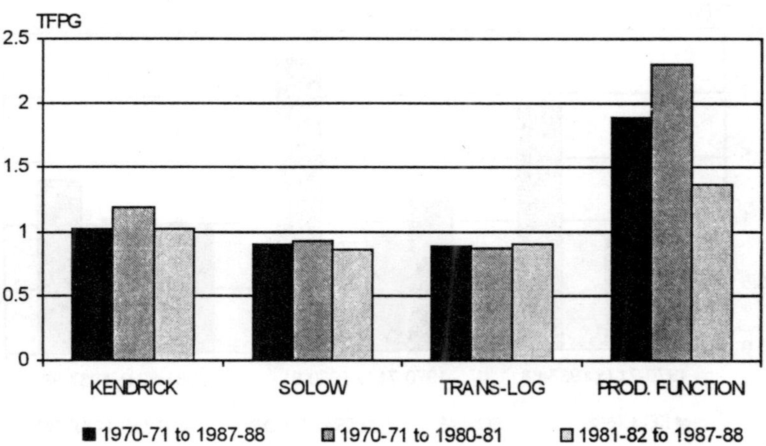

Average Annual TFPG (Var. Y)
All Industries

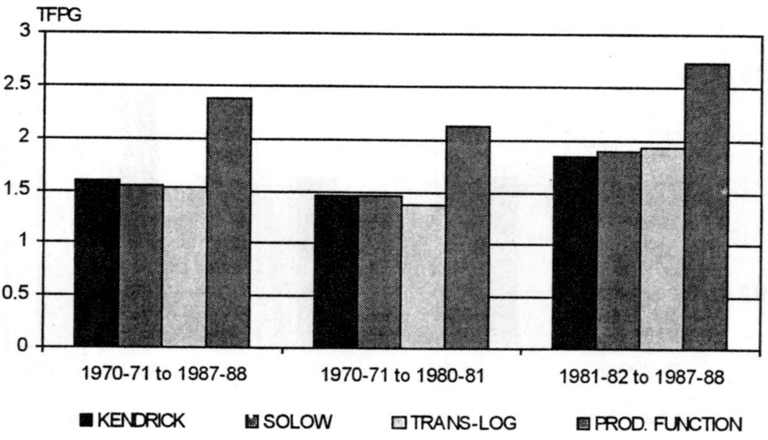

Average Annual TFPG (Var. Z)
All Industries

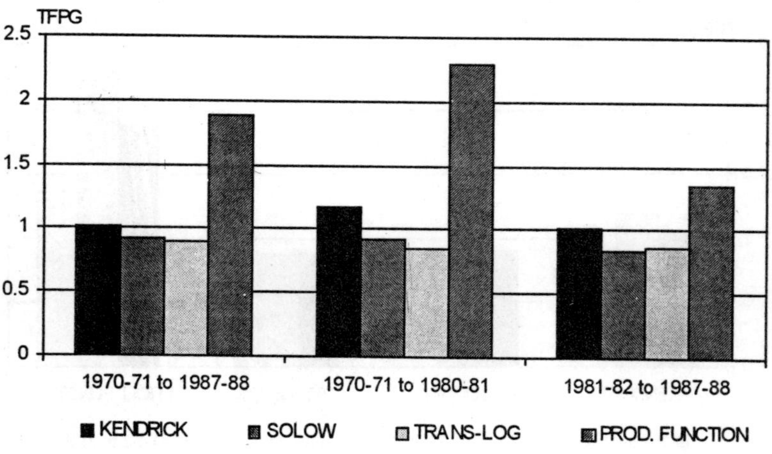

Contributions of TFPG and Input Growth
All Industries (Var. Y)

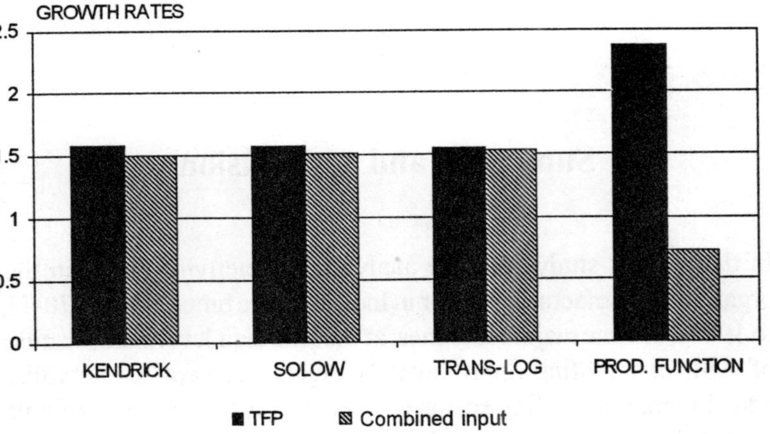

Contributions of TFPG and Input Growth
All Industries (Var. Z)

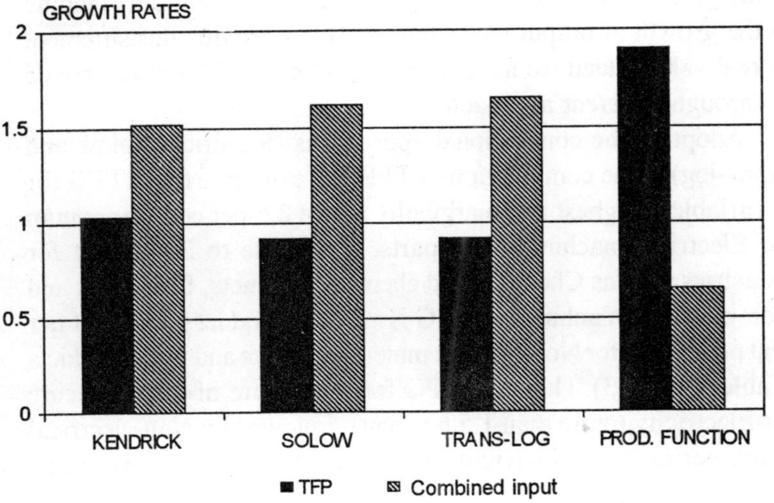

6

Summary and Conclusion

In the present study we have analysed productivity trends in the organised manufacturing sector in India over the time period 1970-71 to 1987-88. Nine major industries, at the two-digit level classification of ASI, constituting approximately eighty per cent of the value added in manufacturing sector in 1982-83 (at current prices) have been taken up for this study. We have computed total factor productivity growth (TFPG) using the conventional approaches as well as through the estimation of production function. Our estimates of production functions are obtained from the general trans-log form through the process of backward elimination and after subjecting the estimates to a three-fold test. The tests relate to observational 'robustness', joint insignificance of excluded terms of the general trans-log form and positivity of contribution of inputs to the growth of output (see Chapter 2). As regards measurement of real value added we have used two estimates, Y and Z, arrived at through different approaches.

Adopting the conventional approaches (Kendrick, Solow and Trans-log) in the computation of TFPG, we observe that TFPG for Y variable is highest and marginally above 2.5 per cent per annum for Electrical machinery and parts. It is close to 2 per cent for industries such as Chemical and chemical products, Electricity and Non-electrical machinery. TFPG is very low and less than half per cent per annum for Non-metallic mineral products and Food products (Table 3.1, Ch.3). Highest TFPG for Z-measure of output occurs for Electricity (more than 1.5 per cent), followed by Non-electrical machineries and Electrical machinery and parts. It is, thus, significant to note that industries such as Electricity, Electrical machinery and parts and Non-electrical machineries show high growth rates of total factor productivity, for both the measures of real value added. In general for all the nine industries the three measures of TFPG (Kendrick, Solow, Trans-log) produced very close results for each of the measures of real value-added (Table 3.1, Ch.3).

When we consider TFPG for the two sub-periods (1970-71 to 1980-81 and 1981-82 to 1987-88) it is observed that Kendrick on the one hand and Solow and Trans-log on the other, do not always project the same picture with regard to changes in TFPG between the sub-periods. However, magnitude of divergence is not very large when we consider the aggregate of nine industries (roughly referred to as the aggregate manufacturing sector). Broadly, it seems that for the manufacturing sector as a whole, Kendrick, Solow and Trans-log measures show a close resemblance with regard to their behaviour over the sub-periods (Table 3.2, Ch. 3).

Ranking of industries according to TFPG for various approaches (Kendrick, Solow and Trans-log) are almost the same for each of the value added indices used (rank correlation coefficients are very close to unity). Thus, it seems that the ranking of industries according to their TFPG is practically independent of the measures of TFPG adopted. However, our results also show that ranking based on average annual TFPG for various indices does in fact, to a certain extent depend on the measurement of value added index. We may note that, in general TFPG is high for variable Y compared to variable Z. This seems to be the result of high growth rate of output obtained from the Y-measure of output compared to Z-measure.

It is interesting to note that our estimates of TFPG for the overall manufacturing sector for all the conventional measures (Kendrick, Solow and Trans-log) for the period 1970-71 to 1980-81, for variable Y show close matching with the corresponding estimates of Goldar (1986), (Table 3.3,Ch.3), though Goldar's capital stock was different and the coverage in terms of time and industries was also a bit different. As regards the turnaround hypothesis

(Ahluwalia 1991) with respect to the TFPG in Indian manufacturing sector it seems that, our estimates for the Y variable give partial support for the hypothesis, though Z variable does not speak the same. In fact, both the measures of real value added, Y and Z, indicate that there was significant TFPG during the 70s as well as the 80s. This is contrary to Ahluwalia's findings.

The feeling that the assumption of equality between factor shares in output and respective factor elasticities as particularly inappropriate for the Indian economy led us to take up the production function approach to the measurement of TFPG. Though several researchers have adopted this technique, we have deviated from other studies to a significant extent as regards the methodology used (Ch.2).

We have normally obtained more than one estimate of production function for each industry. It is highly significant that all the five regressions for variable Y passing all the tests mentioned earlier, for Chemical and chemical products and for Non-metallic mineral products show very close average annual TFPG. Other industries with normally two regressions (Table 4.2, Ch. 4), also present the same picture with minor exceptions. Z variable also gives similar results. This is definitely encouraging for the TFPG estimates obtained through the production function approach.

High TFPG (around 3 per cent) for variable Y is obtained for industries—Electricity, Chemical and chemical products, Basic metal and alloy and Non-electrical machinery. Very low (less than 0.7 per cent) TFPG occurs for Cotton textiles and Food products. Though Electricity for variable Z also shows high TFPG (approximately 3 per cent), it ranks next to Transport equipment and parts where TFPG is marginally above 3.5 per cent. As in the case of variable Y, Cotton textiles and Food products again turn up with very low TFPG for variable Z. Interesting finding is that TFPG comes out to be negative for Cotton textiles.

In spite of the fact that the measures of real value added, Y and Z, vary a great deal, interestingly enough, we have found that the ranking of industries based on average annual TFPG obtained from the estimation of production function are not very dissimilar for the two measures of real value added. The rank correlation coefficient between the rankings according to TFPG for variable Y and Z comes out to be 0.78. It also signifies that in spite of the similarity the estimates of TFPG in fact depend on the measurement of the value added index.

So far as the contribution of TFPG and growth in inputs (jointly) towards output growth is concerned, our estimates suggest that the contribution of TFPG (from production function approach) is far greater than that of inputs towards the growth in output. This result is supported by both the measures of real value added. In fact, both the measures of real value added suggest that TFPG (by the production function approach) contributes two-thirds of the growth of value added in the manufacturing sector (Table 4.10, Ch.4).

Partial labour productivity (Ch. 5) shows positive and significant trend for all the industries and for both the variables Y and Z with one exception in case of variable Z. Significant trend is not observed in case of Cotton textiles (for variable Z). In fifty per cent of the cases (for Y and Z together) capital productivity (Ch. 5) presents a significantly positive trend. Interestingly, Cotton textiles (for variable Z) turns up with a significantly negative trend in partial capital productivity.

So far as the average annual TFPG is concerned, significant disparities among the estimates obtained from different approaches are observed. The estimates from Solow and Trans-log measures of TFPG are very close, and they do not deviate very much from the Kendrick measure for both the variables Y and Z. Great divergence is noticed when the above estimates are compared with the corresponding estimates obtained through production function approach.

Though Kendrick measure shows a resemblance with Solow and Trans-log measures for the entire period of our study, it is not exactly true with regard to changes in TFPG between the sub-periods. In case of our regression analysis, we normally obtain more or less similar changes in TFPG over the sub-periods for alternative regressions for the same industry and same measure of output. However, similarity is not very striking when we compare the pictures with regard to changes in TFPG over the sub-periods obtained from the production function approach and the conventional approaches.

In a broad perspective, for the manufacturing sector as a whole, regression analysis turns up with significantly high contribution (three-fourths) from TFPG towards growth of output. Other estimates of TFPG obtained from conventional approaches for variable Y explains fifty per cent of the growth in output. However, it is less than fifty per cent for variable Z. Thus only when Z-measure of output is used to obtain TFPG from the conventional approaches we find the contribution of input growth to be higher than TFPG to the growth of output.

Perfectly indentical ranking according to TFPG obtained through production function approach is observed for industries such as Electrical machinery and parts, Non-metallic mineral products, Food products Cotton textiles (Table 5.5, Ch. 5) for both the variables Y and Z. Very close results, as regards rankings from all the measures of TFPG are observed only for two industries : (i) Electricity, which has a rank either one or two, and (ii) Non-metallic mineral products, which has a rank either 7 or 8 or 9. Notable finding is that Cotton textiles ranked last with regard to average annual TFPG in case of variable Z, for all the measures of TFPG.

Undoubtedly, our study shows that Electricity is the leading industry, possessing significantly high TFPG (Tables 3.1, 4.2 and 4.3, Chs. 3 and 4). Above statement is true for both conventional and production function approach s to the measurement of TFPG and also for both the measures of value added, Y and Z. It is closely followed by Non-electrical machinery and Chemical and Chemical Products. On the other hand, Non-metallic mineral products, Food products and Cotton textiles show low TFPG for most of the measures. It should be noted here that so far as the production function approach is concerned, industries with high TFPG had, almost invariably, low contribution from growth in inputs.

As in the conventional approach, the production function

approach adopted by us also shows that TFPG was higher during the second sub-period compared to the first when we consider the Y-measure of output. But this conclusion is not supported by the Z-measure of output. In any case for both the measures of output and for all the approaches to the measure of TFPG, TFPG was quite significant during the first sub-period. We have noted earlier that Z is a particularly crude measure of real value added and so we are inclined to rely more on the results based on the Y variable. Nevertheless, the similarity of the results obtained through the production function approach by using Y and Z variables are noteworthy. We may repeat that the rankings of industries on the basis of TFPG for the two measures of real value added are to some extent similar and both the variables explain an almost similar proportion (three-fourths) of output growth as the contribution of TFPG.

From our results it appears that the total factor productivity or the residual factor plays a very important role in the growth of the registered manufacturing sector of India. While one is not absolutely certain about what the residual is composed of, the term residual is supposed to mean that it captures whatever is not captured by the growth of capital and labour. In our view the substantial growth of total factor productivity for the registered manufacturing sector of India indicates that during the 70s and the 80s the manufacturing sector witnessed significant technical progress. This observation does not seem to be wide away from commonsense. Because during the two decades the Indian industry underwent quite some diversification and technological sophistication reflected in the rise in the share of manufacturing in GDP and change in the composition of exports in favour of manufacturing.

Appendix

Note: The following tables present data used for computations in the present work. Output and Capital are measured in rupees lakhs. Labour is the weighted sum of 'workers' and 'other employees'.

Table A.1: Output, Capital, Labour
Chemical and Chemical Products

Year	*Y*	*Z*	*K*	*L*
1973-74	107319.68	125702.95	283018.43	434336.54
1974-75	109989.86	148091.92	268533.82	447840.31
1975-76	121422.83	157453.66	308800	497783.59
1976-77	137605.82	164583.46	307988.65	517064.23
1977-78	159429.43	175587.9	350881.79	585839.54
1978-79	180050.13	215645.89	367243.4	599086.75
1979-80	202554.46	205479.7	420763.22	708547.54
1981-82	215720	215720	401484	671155.95
1982-83	233051.76	231121.3	365318.18	691524.23
1983-84	255517.28	270238.67	431339.06	715140.44
1984-85	277609.21	258553.7	418233.49	728707.59
1985-86	297912.51	266988.91	460759.45	750112.79
1986-87	322191.53	263570.34	486622.72	729549.81
1987-88	345713.74	301047.8	503332.69	774386.89

Table A.2: Output, Capital, Labour
Electricity

Year	*Y*	*Z*	*K*	*k*
1973-74	117802.10	98177.02	1098023.0	651219.96
1974-75	120273.73	89535.66	941669.1	614080.15
1975-76	139085.98	124406.50	863508.2	638712.71
1976-77	158294.58	136098.01	1035935.2	681309.21
1977-78	170103.26	160139.77	1357068.7	763795.37
1978-79	187047.27	211711.05	1473841.6	784930.27
1979-80	192404.74	189019.68	1454438.3	840528.90
1980-81	227954.28	188194.05	1467642.1	918861.15
1981-82	264928.00	264928.00	1494923.0	911652.43
1982-83	282801.19	264458.34	1642899.1	958393.72
1983-84	345581.92	350203.59	1747273.8	1038990.60
1984-85	330602.96	263955.45	1893724.6	1134710.80
1985-86	334861.75	272918.64	1827895.4	991246.05
1986-87	401316.73	342929.31	1922294.8	1020632.90
1987-88	423669.18	317555.13	2170271.3	1079590.10

Table A.3: Output, Capital, Labour
Basic Metal and Alloy

Year	*Y*	*Z*	*K*	*L*
1973-74	100587.63	105071.96	307536.87	534129.19
1974-75	106606.67	122824.09	233605.12	502888.95
1975-76	122105.89	139736.59	380586.89	581735.95
1976-77	129761.25	148124.04	417262.56	569781.59
1977-78	138760.34	129792.51	444963.26	595367.23
1978-79	162789.21	166168.56	446652.49	655837.26
1979-80	165156.03	157071.34	469976.07	658287.97
1980-81	177827.94	169480.71	486370.33	677572.43
1981-82	203969	203968	519227	703215.88
1982-83	225774.05	195423.04	550959.09	709834.83
1983-84	213174.51	210814.37	603319.31	761278.36
1984-85	231499.13	197691.33	655489.53	801300.12
1985-86	220757.03	224136.83	604851.02	694271.55
1986-87	243824.72	192736.66	593414.47	722956.38
1987-88	257765.2	215509.88	668694.66	726101.32

Table A.4: Output, Capital, Labour
Transport Equipment and Parts

Year	*Y*	*Z*	*K*	*L*
1970-71	67807.97	60894.47	82831.4	449733.06
1971-72	72215.03	68883.33	79850.42	454131.84
1973-74	80802.79	65250.92	81370.97	458385.56
1974-75	77388.99	70218.7	70559.42	465021.81
1975-76	75021.77	72525.2	67783.61	423200.25
1976-77	87060.92	79093.42	80628.85	411156.96
1977-78	88395.87	78706.05	85354.63	432301.42
1978-79	101617.95	102548.16	180331.38	471239.96
1979-80	108116.85	106718.33	167992.44	576446.95
1980-81	114230.39	110329.66	155595.7	576785.93
1981-82	126909	126909	151322	597776.79
1982-83	137621.7	138546.78	155005.45	606603.22
1983-84	141890.66	136541.49	157141.63	601490.01
1984-85	155965.63	142167.86	182632.05	624789.89
1985-86	154862.21	130514.79	178854.65	564288.72
1986-87	175526.81	148950.8	188833.67	578895.36
1987-88	188646.92	142030.59	203268.07	575088.03

Table A.5: Output, Capital, Labour
Electrical Machinery and Parts

Year	*Y*	*Z*	*K*	*L*
1970-71	37476.78	51444.72	93633.72	272229
1971-72	42038.03	57114.28	89994.46	287483
1973-74	52667.31	64247.23	71096.77	324100
1974-75	48290.18	67386.69	75065.81	329023
1975-76	54546.57	80304.06	70836.07	341223
1976-77	65084.42	79566.62	75038.9	349635
1977-78	70103.89	82495.67	79686.9	360102
1978-79	74975.47	88624.65	78123.17	376520
1979-80	82220.96	93275.52	78532.75	414007
1980-81	95622.47	99852.26	80147.23	419973
1981-82	97728	97728	77444	417404
1982-83	117766.01	120535.68	90855.46	442159
1983-84	113427.56	122060.74	99124.46	445469
1984-85	127385.4	148606.21	107359.9	467995
1985-86	134238.32	122494.08	107010.9	465625
1986-87	142275.25	127530.84	110075.73	448448
1987-88	176533.53	157611.85	138872.68	500510

Table A.6: Output, Capital, Labour
Non Electrical Machinery

Year	*Y*	*Z*	*K*	*L*
1969-70	48980.06	51900.76	85637.77	359121.5
1970-71	52215.08	55248.74	78674.42	365204.7
1971-72	56852.44	61228.57	85734.07	389332.2
1973-74	61763.86	62797.04	80000	407478.5
1974-75	71537.82	75196.51	79537.48	424758.4
1975-76	72102.55	84495.94	83845.9	436688.7
1976-77	85567.01	96600.31	89914.1	446719.9
1977-78	92042.12	96946.69	99862.62	500120.6
1978-79	98196.02	103658.64	93719.94	498501.7
1979-80	101705.2	102774.91	94831.23	551145.1
1980-81	108949.93	107808.16	89702.15	514711.9
1981-82	115713	115713	95934	553417.5
1982-83	124497.17	123524.86	101371.82	558707.5
1983-84	133053.41	135357.57	124539.06	579329.4
1984-85	140177.75	149764.52	117542.67	553874.3
1985-86	150056.69	154409.02	146383.72	571209.02
1986-87	147078.42	135663.89	118790.4	528824.1
1987-88	168925.65	142672.4	126394.11	574644.4

Table A.7: Output, Capital, Labour
Non-Metallic Mineral Products

Year	*Y*	*Z*	*K*	*L*
1970-71	30107.06	34148.24	72494.19	318189
1971-72	30804.96	35207.14	71603.88	319869
1973-74	33374.53	31636.53	67873.27	351984.5
1974-75	31321.93	32974.64	57137.11	353420
1975-76	33767.21	41045.53	58931.15	366825.5
1976-77	37935.7	42787.14	63494.33	370831.5
1977-78	41823.34	48965.42	64498.4	385395
1978-79	41811.17	51032.58	68552.79	453897
1979-80	41514.39	49523.99	67110.83	435447
1980-81	44001.15	51801.54	77907.14	426070
1981-82	48332	56087	90097	455180
1982-83	55835.74	78148.46	107026.36	507561
1983-84	58295.42	86174.51	142826.61	536408
1984-85	65363.04	96522.67	144838.16	514917
1985-86	74866.27	103160.5	189881.54	533434
1986-87	78632.67	90559.95	222096.69	524354
1987-88	83494.24	98003.82	243982.09	532512.5

Table A.8: Output, Capital, Labour
Cotton Textiles

Year	*Y*	*Z*	*K*	*L*
1973-74	99903.4	145267.53	109907.83	1059023.9
1974-75	111904.72	142725.83	101694.7	1165787.9
1975-76	120856.75	122300.81	99340.98	1174812.2
1976-77	126274.48	124315.47	106249.59	1162232.4
1977-78	133352.73	139440.92	116995.21	1177304.7
1978-79	147774.3	176328.61	121612.9	1228620.3
1979-80	140103.99	175134.07	118437.03	1248457.7
1980-81	139432.83	160125.69	126331.82	1174078.5
1981-82	134151	134151	122690	1120616.9
1982-83	141472.21	122629.29	140730	1158820.8
1983-84	152830.1	148327.63	159169.96	1128414.3
1984-85	154955.43	128207.64	163165.86	1045142.2
1985-86	159546.2	128198.96	163482.56	972078.4
1986-87	151714.78	134536.38	158528.74	980794.8
1987-88	159859.3	121059.27	148157.39	917941.9

Table A.9: Output, Capital, Labour
Food Products

Year	*Y*	*Z*	*K*	*L*
1970-71	89951.22	77992.46	111476.74	818361.1
1973-74	66956.2	68507.38	108546.08	862703.6
1974-75	78925.65	78738.51	101250.46	1181532.4
1975-76	91603.9	87196.74	104506.56	1364960.7
1976-77	94487.36	96453.29	116554.29	1461386.1
1977-78	114724.14	108693.08	139461.66	1545844.2
1978-79	145518.38	104701.13	142131.96	1450210.6
1979-80	117195.97	105193.11	142341.31	1535404.6
1980-81	86791.6	92291.07	136926.39	1672760.5
1981-82	108782	108782	132405	1716361.4
1982-83	137179.7	126156.98	135751.82	1566134.7
1983-84	134774.67	160963.22	164257.51	1276321.1
1984-85	136950.21	151581.54	163698.07	1289441.3
1985-86	144217.31	152821.01	159757.13	1218031.9
1986-87	148101.92	157300.07	170150.78	1184577.6
1987-88	166132.73	167220.52	179686.5	1266891.8

Bibliography

Abramovitz, M. (1956), "Resources and Output Trends in the United States since 1870", *American Economic Review* 46, no. 2 (May) : 5-23.

Ahluwalia, I. J. (1985), *Industrial Growth in India - Stagnation since Mid-sixties*, Oxford University Press, New Delhi.

Ahluwalia, I. J. (1991), *Productivity Growth in Indian Manufacturing*, Oxford University Press, New Delhi.

Balakrishnan, P. and Pushpangadan, K. (1994), "TFPG in Manufacturing Industry : A Fresh Look", *Economic and Political Weekly*, July 30.

Banerji, A. (1975), *Capital Intensity and Productivity in Indian Industry*, Macmillan, Delhi.

Brahmananda, P.R. (1982), *Productivity in the Indian Economy : Rising Inputs for Falling Outputs*, Himalaya Publishing House, Bombay.

Berndt, E.R. and Christensen, L.R. (1973), "The Translog Function and the Substitution of Equipment Structure and Labour in U.S. Manufacturing 1929-68", *Journal of Econometrics*, no. 1, March.

Bruno, M. (1984), "Raw Materials, Profits and the Productivity Slowdown", *Quarterly Journal of Economics*, no.1.

Bruton, H.J. (1967), "Productivity Growth in Latin America", *American Economic Review*, December.

Burmeister, E., and Dobell, A.R. (1970), *Mathematical Theories of Economic Growth*, The Macmillan Company, Collier-Macmillan, London.

Central Statistical Organisation (1989), *Sources and Methods: National Accounts Statistics*, Government of India, New Delhi.

Central Statistical Organisation (1991), *National Accounts Statistics*, Government of India, New Delhi.

Central Statistical Organisation, *Annual Survey of Industries*, various issues, Government of India.

Chambers, R.C. (1988), *Applied Production Analysis*, Cambridge University Press, Cambridge.

Christensen, L.R. and Jorgenson, D.W. (1970), "U.S. Real Product and Real Factor Input, 1929-1967", Reviews of Income and Wealth, March.

Christensen, L.R., Jorgenson, D.W. and Lau, L.J. (1971), "Conjugate Duality and the Transcendental Logarithmic Production Function", *Econometrica*, vol. 39, no. 4.

Christensen, L.R., Jorgenson, D.W. and Lau, L.J. (1973), "Transcendental Logarithmic Production Frontiers", *Review of Economics and Statistics,* February.

Christensen, L.R., Cummings, D. and Jorgenson, D.W. (1980), "Economic Growth, 1947-1973, An International Comparison", in Kendrick, J.W. and Vaccara, B.(eds.), *New Developments in Productivity Measurement,* University of Chicago Press, Chicago.

Denison, E.F. (1957), "Theoretical Aspects of Quality Change, Capital Consumption and Net Capital Formation", *NBER Studies in Income and Wealth*, Princeton University Press, 215-61.

Denison, E.F. (1967), *Why Growth Rates Differ : Post war experiences in nine western countries,* The Brookings Institution, Washington D.C.

Denison, E.F. (1974), *Accounting for United States Economic Growth, 1929-1969*, The Brookings Institution, Washington D.C.

Desai, M. (1979), *Applied Econometrics*, Tata McGraw-Hill Publishing Company Limited, New Delhi.

Diewert, W.E. (1978), 'Hicks Aggregation Theorem and the Existence of a Real Value Added Function, in *Production Economics : A Dual Approach to Theory and Application*, edited by Fuss, M. and McFadden, D., 2:17-52. Amsterdam, North Holland.

Diewert, W.E. (1980), Aggregation Problems in the Measurement of Capital, *The Measurement of Capital* ed. Dan Usher, 433-528, University of Chicago Press, Chicago.

Dhar, P.N. (1988) 'The Indian Economy: Past Performance and Current Issues', R.E.B. Lucas and G.F. Papanek (eds.), *The Indian Economy : Recent Development and Future Prospects*, Delhi, Oxford University Press.

Divisia, F. (1925), "L'indice monetaire et la theorie de la monnaie". *Revue d'economie politique*, 39e Annee, no. 4 (July-August) : 842-61; no. 5 (September-October) : 980-1008; no. 6 (November-December) : 1121-51.

Draper, N.R. and Smith, H. (1966), *Applied Regression Analysis*, John Wiley and Sons, Inc.

Dutt, R.C., (1987), *Public Enterprises in India: Their Genesis and Perspective,* Centre for Studies in Public Enterprise Management Monograph Series : I. Indian Institute of Management, Calcutta.

Fabricant, S. (1954), "Economic Progress and Economic Change", *Report of the National Bureau of Economic Research,* New York.

Garegnani, P. (1972), "Heterogeneous Capital, Production Function and the Theory of Distributions", reprinted in Hunt, E.K.& Schwartz, J.G. (eds), *A Critique of Economic Theory*, Penguine Education.

Goldar, B.N. (1986), *Productivity Growth in Indian Industry*, Allied Publishers, New Delhi.

Goldsmith, R.W. (1951), "A Perpetual Inventory of National Wealth", *Studies in Income and Wealth*, Vol. 14, NBER.

Gollop, F.M. and Jorgenson, D.W. (1980), 'U.S. Productivity Growth by Industry 1947-73', *New Developments in Productivity Measurements and Analysis*, edited by Kendrick and Vaccara, NBER.

Griliches, Z. (1967), 'Production Functions in Manufacturing: Some Preliminary Results', *The Theory and Empirical Analysis of Production*, edited by M. Brown, NBER.

Hashim, B.R. and Dadi, M.M. (1973), *Capital-Output Relations in Indian Manufacturing (1946-64)*, M.S. University of Baroda, Baroda.

Hodges, D., (1969), "A Note on Estimation of Cobb-Douglas and CES Production Function Models", *Econometrics*, October.

Jorgenson, D.W. and Griliches, Z. (1967), "The Explanation of Productivity Change", *Review of Economic Studies,* July.

Jorgenson, D.W. and Griliches, Z. (1972), "Issues in Growth Accounting A Reply to Edward F. Denison", *Survey of Current Business*, May.

Jorgenson, D.W. (1991), "Productivity and Economic Growth", in Berndt, E. and Triplet, (eds.).

Joshi, V. and Little, I.M.D. (1994), *India: Macroeconomics and Political Economy 1964-1991*, Oxford University Press, Delhi.

Kaldor, N. (1966), *Causes of the Slow Rate of Growth of the United Kingdom,* Cambridge University Press, Cambridge.

Kendrick, J.W. (1961), *Productivity Trends in the United States*, NBER.

Kendrick, J.W. (1973), "Post War Productivity Trends in the United States, 1949-1969", *NBER*, New York.

Kennedy, C. and Thirwall, A.P. (1972), "Surveys in Applied Economics: Technical Progress", *Economic Journal*, March.

Kmenta, J. (1967), "On the Estimation of CES Production Function", *International Economic Review*, No. 8, June.

Krishna, K.L. (1987), 'Industrial Growth and Productivity in India', Brahmananda P.R. and Panchamukhi, V.R. edited, *The Development Process of the Indian Economy*, Himalaya Publishing House.

Kumari, A. (1993) "Productivity in Public Sector", *Economic and Political Weekly*, Nov. 27.

Labour Bureau, *Indian Labour Statistics*, Various Issues, Government of India.

Little, I.M.D., Majumdar, D. and Page, J.M. Jr. (1987), *Small Manufacturing Enterprises*, World Bank Research Publication, Oxford University Press, New York.

Maddala, G.S. (1992), *Introduction to Econometrics*, second edition, Macmillan Publishing Company, New York.

Margit, S., and Singh, N., (1995), 'Technology and Indian Industry', Mookherjee, D., edited *Indian Industry, Policies and Performance*, Oxford University Press.

Mehta, S.S. (1980), *Productivity, Production Function and Technical Change,* Concept Publishing Company, New Delhi.

Nadiri, M. I. (1970), "Some Approaches to the Theory and Measurement of Total Factor Productivity: A Survey", *Journal of Economic Literature,* Vol VIII.

Nadiri, M. I. (1972), "International Studies of Factor Inputs and Total Factor Productivity : A Brief Survey", *Review of Income and Wealth*, June.

Narasimham, G.V.L. and Fabrycy, M.Z. (1974), "Relative Efficiencies of Organised Industries in India, 1948-58", *Journal of Development Studies*, January.

Nelson, R.R. (1981), "Research on Productivity Growth and Productivity Differences: Dead Ends and New Departures", *Journal of Economic Literature,* September

Panchamukhi, V.R. (1986), *Capital Formation and Output in the Third World*, Radient, Delhi.

Pindyck, R.S. and Rubinfeld, D.L. (1976), *Econometric Models and Economic Forecasts*, McGraw-Hill Kogakusha Ltd.

Raj, K.N. (1976), "Growth and Stagnation in Indian Industrial Development", *Economic and Political Weekly*, November, 26.

Raj Krishna and Mehta, S.S. (1968), "Productivity Trends in the Large Scale Industries", *Economic and Political Weekly*, October, 26.

Reddy, M.G.K. and Rao, S.V. (1962), "Functional Distribution in the Large Scale Manufacturing Sector in India", *Artha Vijnana*, 4.

Reserve Bank of India, *Report of Currency and Finance*, Various issues, Government of India.

Robinson, J. (1972), "Capital Theory Upto Date" in Hunt, E.K. & Schwartz, J.G. (eds.), *A Critique of Economic Theory*, Penguine Education.

Rowthorn, R. (1975), "What Remains of Kaldor's Law?", *Economic Journal*, March.

Sankar, U. (1970), "Elasticity of Substitution and Returns to Scale in Indian Manufacturing Industries", *International Economic Review*, Vol. II.

Sastry, V.S.R.K. (1966), "Measurement of Productivity and Production Function in Sugar Industry in India 1951-1961", *Indian Journal of Industrial Relations*, July.

Schmookler, J. (1952), "The Changing Efficiency of the American Economy 1869-1938", *Review of Economics and Statistics*, August.

Shivmaggi, Rajgopalan and Venkatachalam (1968), "Wages, Labour Productivity and Costs of Production", *Economic and Political Weekly*, May 4.

Sinha, J.N. and Sawhney, P.K. (1970), *Wages and Productivity in Indian Industries*, Vikas Publications, Delhi.

Solow, R.M. (1957), "Technical Change and the Aggregate Production Function", *Review of Economics and Statistics*, August.

Syrquin, M. (1984), "Resource Allocation and Productivity Growth" in *Economic Structure and Performance*, Essays in Honour of Chenery H.B., Academic Press.

Tinbergen, J. (1942), Zur Theorie der Langfristigen Wirtschaftsentwicklung, *Weltwirtschaftliches Archiv* 55, No.1.

Zellner, A., Kmenta, J. and Dreze, J., (1966), "Specification and Estimation of Cobb-Douglas Production Function Models," *Econometrica*, October.

INDEX